ANGELS

FROM GENESIS
TO REVELATION

First printing—February 1997—5,000 copies

ANGELS FROM GENESIS TO REVELATION
Copyright © 1997 by N. W. Hutchings and Bob Glaze

Printed in the United States of America

Published by:
Hearthstone Publishing, Ltd.
500 Beacon Drive • Oklahoma City, OK 73127
(405) 787-4055 • (800) 580-2604 • FAX (405) 787-2589

ISBN 1-57558-013-6

ANGELS

FROM GENESIS TO REVELATION

Dr. N.W. HUTCHINGS
AND
BOB GLAZE

Table of Contents

Introduction

If we believe that the Bible is the inspired, inerrant Word of God, which we must believe, then we also must believe in the literal existence of angels. We are informed in the Scriptures that angels were created by God as free moral beings in that they can obey God or disobey. It is also indicated in Scripture that one-third of the angels rebelled and follow Satan. It can also be known from Scripture that angels inhabit the heavens as servants in the Kingdom of God. The Kingdom of God is indeed a kingdom with angels as subjects divided into different orders: watchers, holy ones, warrior angels, archangels, etc.

In opposition to God and His angels is Satan and his angels. The ambition of Satan has never changed—to exalt his throne above the stars of God. This struggle, this war, will not be concluded until Satan and his angels are cast out of the heavens (Rev. 12).

Angels are spirit beings, but they can materialize with the appearance of men upon either their will or at the command of the Lord. Men and women are less powerful than angels, but in the resurrection, Christians will be more powerful and rule over the angels.

Angels, according to Scripture, were active on earth before the flood. Cherubim were placed to guard the Tree of Life after Adam and Eve sinned. We believe the "sons of God" who married "daughters of men" referred to in the sixth chapter of Genesis, were the angels who left their first estate, took upon themselves the form of men, and cohabited with women. After the flood angels were sent on special assignments as God's messengers to fulfill God's will—Sodom and Gomorrah is one of many examples. Angels were very evident during the ministry of Jesus Christ, because He was offering the Kingdom of God to Israel at that time. However, after the thirteenth chapter of Acts when the offer of the Kingdom to Israel was set aside and the Apostle Paul was sent to the Gentiles with the gospel of grace to call out of the Gentiles a people for Christ's name (Acts 15), the ministry of angels became less evident.

In this dispensation when God is calling out of the Gentiles a people to complete His Church, Christians are to follow the leading of the indwelling Holy Spirit. The Apostle John wrote his gospel, according to most biblical chronologists, in A.D. 90, and he mentioned angels only four times in casual references, and not once in his three epistles. Yet, in the Revelation, John made sixty-eight references to angels. Why? Because in the Revelation the Church has been translated, the Holy Spirit is taken out of the world with the Church, the Kingdom of God on earth is apparent and imminent, and angels will busily carry out the judgment determined to reclaim this planet and establish the Lord God as King of kings upon the throne of David.

Today, dozens of books are being written about angels. Christians are being instructed that each one has a guardian angel. It is being taught that each child has a guardian angel, even though one and one-half million Jewish children died in the Holocaust and thousands of children are being killed or sexually molested each day. This does not mean that angels do not or cannot intervene in certain people's lives today, but according to Scripture, this is by special assignment and not by divine entitlement. The undue stress today on the importance of angelic influence in the lives of Christians practically amounts to the worship of angels, which is strictly forbidden by God (Col. 2:18; Rev. 22:8–9).

It is our prayer that this humble effort on the study of angels will at least provide the reader with a correct dispensational overview of the ministry of angels as presented in Scripture from Genesis to Revelation.

I.

Nature of Angels

How do we know that there are angels out there ministering and trafficking in the heavens, serving God? How do we know that angels really exist?

If you asked the average person on the street if he believed in angels, the majority would say, "Well, absolutely." However, most people have a distorted view of what angels really are, and what they really do. Most believe that angels have wings with which they fly, but we do not see that in the majority of angels in Scripture. There are angels in the Scriptures that do have wings, and this will be discussed later. However, we should stick to what the Bible says about angels, and not what the man on the street says about angels.

The word "angel," or a form of the word "angel," is mentioned almost three hundred times in Scripture in some nineteen different books, so it can be seen that the writers of both the Old and New Testaments believed in angels. Since they are mentioned almost three hundred times, we know that the Bible *teaches* that angels exist.

What is an angel? An angel in the Bible—the Old Testament Hebrew word as well as the New Testament Greek word—simply means "a messenger," and they serve the one who rules them. That is their job assignment. They are just messengers. They carry messages from their master to men or other angels. Angels are only interested in one thing: serving their master, either good or bad.

We know that there are fallen angels and angels who have remained true to their created order. But, when were angels created? Did they always exist, or were they coexistent with God? How were they created, and who created them?

Insight to these questions is found in Job 38. This is probably the only place in Scripture that we really find a definitive time of their creation. Most believe that they were created beginning with the first day of Genesis creation, but we do not see this in the book of Job. In Job 38:4–7 we read this:

> Where wast thou when I laid the foundations of the earth? declare, if thou hast understanding. Who hath laid the measures thereof, if thou knowest? or who hath stretched the line upon it? Whereupon are the foundations thereof fastened? or who laid the corner stone thereof; When the morning stars sang together, and all the sons of God shouted for joy?

God is asking Job: "Where were you before the foundation of the earth? You weren't here when I created the earth, and you were not here present with the angels as they shouted for joy at the time of creation." It can be seen that the creation of angels took place prior to the creation of this earth. They already existed, and joined with God in a celebration of this creation.

Who created the angels? We know that all things were created by Christ, as stated in Colossians 1:16–17 where Paul says:

> For by him were all things created, that are in heaven, and that are in earth, visible and invisible, whether they

be thrones, or dominions, or principalities, or powers: all things were created by him, and for him: And he is before all things, and by him all things consist.

Christ not only created the earth as we know it, but He also created the heavens and put the angels in them. So, Christ is the Creator, and angels are part of the creation prior to the creation of the earth.

Does the Bible give any information as to how many angels there are? The Bible has much to say about multitudes of angels, but we are not told their exact number. Some idea of the number is given in Revelation 5:11 where it says:

And I beheld, and I heard the voice of many angels round about the throne and the beasts and the elders: and the number of them was ten thousand times ten thousand, and thousands of thousands.

That can be understood as being millions. Also, Matthew 26:53 reports where Christ said that he could call down thirty-six to seventy-two thousand angels. So, we know that there are many, many angels; they are innumerable. Daniel 7:10 mentions that there are millions of angels (". . . thousand thousands ministered unto him, and ten thousand times ten thousand stood before him . . ."). How many angels there are is really not known—perhaps as many as the grains of sand on the shore.

There is an enormous universe out in space, and the Kingdom of God is a kingdom. God rules over His kingdom and the angels are His messengers, or His servants. Of course, there are different classifications of angels who have different assignments, different missions, different kinds of service. These aspects will be discussed later. It says in Hebrews 12:22, ". . . an innumerable company of angels." This means that no one is able to number them; no one knows how many there are.

Dr. Emil Gaverluk, a renowned Christian author, suggested that the number of angels who rebelled to follow Satan and leave their created order would be the same number in the Church at the Rapture. We read about the fullness of the Gentiles in Scripture and the translation of the Church. It was Dr. Gaverluk's theory that when the number of the Church (those saved during this dispensation of grace) reached the number of the angels who rebelled and fell, then that would determine the time of the Rapture. There is no particular scripture for that opinion, but it is something of interest to think about.

In Revelation 12 we are told that one-third of the angels—however many that was—followed Lucifer. This means that one-third of the angels are fallen angels.

Many Christians—even non-Christians—have claimed to have seen angels, and some believe that they have guardian angels. How do we know that there are such things as spirits beings? Suppose someone walking by a lake had never seen a fish and knew nothing about them. Although there is no evidence of fish (because they are all beneath the surface), he sees a ripple and wonders what is causing it. Just so, even though we may not see an angel in this life, we know they exist by their ministry.

Consider that until about one hundred and twenty-five years ago no one knew that there was a world of minute organisms, germs, and viruses. If you had told someone back then that they were surrounded by *millions* of microbes, germs, and viruses which were causing some of the illnesses of the day, you would not have been believed. Just because we cannot see angels, or have not seen angels (unless it is God's will that we do so), we do know, according to Scripture and other evidences which will be mentioned in this study, that angels *do* exist. According to the scriptures that have been brought out, they are innumerable, meaning that even our best computer could not number them.

Let us proceed to the nature of angels. What is the nature of angels? What are they like? How powerful are they? Do they die? Do they bear children? Do they procreate? What sex are they?

One of the first things to be understood concerning angels is that they are *not* to be worshiped (Col. 2:18). Paul says that we are not to worship angels, so this must have been a problem even in the New Testament days of the first century. We see in the Old Testament that people had a problem worshipping angels. Some people are starting to worship angels again today. A major theme for Christmas this year (1996) is based on angels. We are asked to believe that they are involved in everything that we do. The New Age movement is heavily involved in the worship of angels. John, in Revelation 22:8–9, also mentions this:

> . . . I fell down to worship before the feet of the angel which shewed me these things. Then saith he unto me, See thou do it not: for I am thy fellowservant. . . .

Angels simply carry out the will of the One that they serve. The fallen angels carry out the will of Satan, and the unfallen angels carry out the will of God. Fallen angels are mentioned in Jude, verse 6:

> And the angels which kept not their first estate, but left their own habitation, he hath reserved in everlasting chains under darkness unto the judgment of the great day.

The angels that "kept not their first estate" (they were created holy), when they left that and followed Lucifer, then they became unholy angels.

Angels are *not* omniscient. They do not know everything. They are not all-knowing like God. Matthew 24:36 quotes Christ speaking of His second coming:

> But of that day and hour knoweth no man, no, not the angels of heaven, but my Father only.

First Peter 1:12 says:

> Unto whom it was revealed, that not unto themselves, but unto us they did minister the things, which are now reported unto you by them that have preached the gospel unto you with the Holy Ghost sent down from heaven; which things the angels desire to look into.

So, the angels are curious about this thing called "salvation." But the angels who fell will never have another opportunity. Satan and the angels who followed him know that their ultimate demise is going to be in the lake of fire. It is something like a man, perhaps, who is convicted of murder and sentenced to death, but escapes from prison. He feels that he has nothing to lose, so he does what he wants to do, and if this involves robbery or murder or some other crime, then he just continues on because his fate is already sealed. However, Satan is not omniscient; angels are not omniscient; they do not know everything. Someone wrote to this ministry asking if angels could read a person's mind. No, angels cannot read a person's mind. They can influence people, but they do not read minds.

We also see that angels are spirit beings. In Hebrews

1:6–7 we read that angels were created as spirits. They do not have a body, as we know it, because they are in a different dimension. The rule is: "If you can see it, it is not eternal; it is only temporal. If you cannot see it, then it is eternal." We cannot see our own souls, spirits, and personalities, because they are eternal. In Luke 20:34–36 we see that they do not die. It is important to remember that *we* do not die; we die in the flesh, but our souls and spirits live on. Then, those "in Christ" which die prior to the Rapture (1 Cor. 15:51–58) will be rejoined to their resurrected bodies. Christ said that some are going to spend eternity in damnation, and others will spend eternity with Him in heaven.

Angels are spirit beings and we cannot see them unless they are revealed to us. We read in Scripture that this has actually happened. There were times, such as with Abraham, at Sodom and Gomorrah, Elijah, and many other places in the Bible, where angels were made visible. So they can, at their will, or at the instruction of the Lord, reveal themselves to us. We have learned that they do not die, even though some of them fell and are reserved to everlasting judgment.

How powerful are they? Supernatural things occur, things that cannot be accounted for or explained. We know that when these superhuman things take place, it is probably not of man. In explaining those things, we are limited to what the Scripture has to say. Our intention is to study what God says about angels and what He is allowing us to know.

II.

Fallen Angels

Angels *do not* die; they live forever. In Luke 20:34–36 Christ addressed the Sadducees about the resurrection (Sadducees did not believe in the resurrection):

> And Jesus answering said unto them, The children of this world marry, and are given in marriage: But they which shall be accounted worthy to obtain that world, and the resurrection from the dead, neither marry, nor are given in marriage: Neither can they die any more: for they are equal unto the angels; and are the children of God, being the children of the resurrection.

We see that in Christ's account of the resurrection, He mentions angels, and how once a person is resurrected he is equal to the angels as far as never dying. So, angels never die. They were created holy; some fell and became unholy, but that does not mean that they are going to disappear. They *will* be punished forever in hell.

We see, too, that they are very powerful. Angels do things that man is incapable of doing as far as strength and his physical abilities are concerned. In 2 Peter 2:11 we read:

> Whereas angels, which are greater in power and might, bring not railing accusation against them before the Lord.

Peter here was talking about some of the other things fallen angels had done. Peter said here, "angels, which are greater in power and might." He was talking about angels being more powerful than men. We really do not know their capabilities. Many things have been ascribed to angels in the Old Testament. We see the angel at Christ's resurrection at the tomb; an angel rolled the stone away. The estimate of the weight of the stone was hundreds of pounds, and one man would not have been capable of moving it, but an angel was able to move it.

However, as we have noted, they are *not* to be worshipped. We read this in both the Old and the New Testaments. Moses said in Exodus 34:14:

> For thou shalt worship no other god: for the LORD, whose name is Jealous, is a jealous God.

God is speaking here about worshipping any thing other than Himself, *including angels!* We also see in the New Testament that Paul speaks about this in Colossians 2:18. Here he is warning the Christians: "Let no man beguile you." (The word "beguile" simply means to set a snare or a net for you.) So, "let no man beguile you of your reward in a voluntary humility and worshipping of angels." We are not to worship angels regardless of how powerful they are, regardless of their stature.

In the Old Testament we see man presented as subservient, more or less, to angels—that they are more powerful than man and above him. In the New Testament we see the reverse. We see that man is placed above the angels, and that is because of the Christian's position in Christ.

The next thing we see is that angels cannot reproduce other angels. It is important that we understand exactly what this means. There has been much discussion concerning Genesis 6. Were the "sons of God" mentioned in Genesis 6 angels, or were they men? In Mark 12:25 we read:

> For when they shall rise from the dead, they neither marry, nor are given in marriage [speaking of people, men and women]; but are as the angels which are in heaven.

Many interpret this scripture to mean that angels cannot cohabitate with men or women, but that is not what this verse is referring to. It refers to marriage. In heaven, Christ tells us, we will not be marrying, we will not be given in marriage. We will all be with Christ, but we will not be as we are today as far as a relationship as husband and wife. The angels in heaven do not have the capacity to marry. In every reference to angels in the Bible, they are referred to in the masculine gender. The angels that are mentioned in Genesis 18:1–2 are referred to in the masculine gender:

> And the LORD appeared unto him in the plains of Mamre: and he sat in the tent door in the heat of the day; And he lift up his eyes and looked, and, lo, three men stood by him: and when he saw them, he ran to meet them from the tent door, and bowed himself toward the ground.

This scripture is speaking of the account of Abraham when three angels came to him. They were represented as being *men*. There is no place in Scripture where we see an angel being represented as a woman or mentioned in the female gender. There are those who believe that Zechariah 5:9 refers to female angels, but that is not the case. It says:

> Then lifted I up mine eyes, and looked, and, behold,
> there came out two women, and the wind was in their
> wings; for they had wings like the wings of a stork: and
> they lifted up the ephah between the earth and the
> heaven.

Zechariah continues in verse 10 to speak to the angel, but
these women were never represented as being angels. If
they could be represented as angels, which they cannot,
they would certainly be evil angels because the stork is an
unclean bird. So we know that those women were not
angels; they were simply symbolic of the conditions that
prevailed.

The leader of the holy angels is Michael, the archangel.
He is the only one that is ever stated in Scripture as being
an archangel. This is revealed in more than one place. In
one instance, Daniel 10:13, the Scripture reads:

> But the prince of the kingdom of Persia withstood me
> one and twenty days: but, lo, Michael, one of the chief
> princes, came to help me; and I remained there with
> the kings of Persia.

This verse refers to Michael as one of the "chief princes,"
which leads us to believe that there is more than one "chief
prince." If there are three "chief princes," then the angels
would probably be divided up among them. We know
that Lucifer has one-third of the fallen angels, and that
Michael is an archangel and he probably carries one-third
of the unfallen angels. Perhaps Gabriel—we don't know—
is another archangel, although Gabriel is never called an
archangel in the Scriptures. This verse says that Michael is
one of the chief princes, and it also speaks of "the prince
of Persia," which could refer to one of the fallen angels.

In Daniel 8:16 we read:

And I heard a man's voice between the banks of Ulai, which called, and said, Gabriel, make this man to understand the vision.

Gabriel is Israel's protector. He is mentioned several times in the Old Testament, including in Daniel 9:21 where it says:

Yea, whiles I was speaking in prayer, even the man Gabriel, whom I had seen in the vision at the beginning, being caused to fly swiftly, touched me about the time of the evening oblation.

Again we see that Gabriel is involved in what Daniel is doing, and certainly Daniel is one of the greatest representatives of Israel in prophecy that we have in Scripture. We see Gabriel in four different verses, and each time he is assigned to Israel.

The other group of angels are the fallen angels, and they are often represented as demons. Scofield believed that the demons that are present today are the spirits of dead men prior to creation or the pre-Adamic race, and they are seeking bodies that they can inhabit to once again carry out the lusts of their own flesh.

Who is the leader of the fallen angels? We read in Revelation 12 about "that old serpent, called the Devil, and Satan," and his angels; Satan is their leader. We know that Satan is a great counterfeiter, and if God has archangels, then doubtless Satan has his own angels who are in charge of doing his dirty work. In Matthew 12:24, we read:

> But when the Pharisees heard it, they said, This fellow
> doth not cast out devils, but by Beelzebub the prince
> of the devils.

Of course, there is a question here whether Beelzebub in that sense was referring to Satan, or to one of the Devil's chief princes. In Revelation 9:11, we read of the demons of the bottomless pit:

> And they had a king over them, which is the angel of
> the bottomless pit, whose name in the Hebrew tongue
> is Abaddon, but in the Greek tongue hath his name
> Apollyon.

Again there is a question here if this is not one of Satan's fallen angels, one of his arch-fallen-angels.

Scofield's theory, mentioned earlier, that demons are spirits of a pre-Adamic race, is difficult to substantiate in Scripture. There are some who believe that when the angels came down, those who willingly left their first estate and took on the form of a man and cohabited with women—which we believe is presented in Genesis 6—that these demons, or souls and spirits of those of whom the angels brought into being through cohabiting with women, were destroyed in the flood. Again, there is a problem substantiating that, so we just have to accept the fact that the demons are doing Satan's dirty work. We cannot be too dogmatic, because we can only be definitive about what is presented to us in Scripture.

III.
Power of Angels

We read in Scripture about Michael, Gabriel, Lucifer, Beelzebub, and Abaddon, so we have to consider this question: Does each angel have a name? We do not know, but it is quite possible. We also read in Scripture that in heaven we will be known as we are. Since some of the angels are specifically called by name in Scripture, then it is more than possible that they all have names.

What about the binding of fallen angels? The fallen angels fall into two groups: the ones who are bound, and the ones who are free. This will be discussed in more depth later. However, in John 8:44—where Christ is addressing those who would seek to kill Him, and He tells them exactly who they represent—we read these words: "Ye are of your father the devil, and the lusts of your father ye will do." Their "father" is none other than Lucifer himself, or Satan as he is also called. The leader of the demons and the fallen angels is Lucifer.

The leader of the demons is called Lucifer in the Old Testament. He was the bright and shining one before pride was found in him and he decided to replace God in the universe. He decided he was going to be king over everything. He was going to exalt *his* authority, his delegated authority, over that which God had given him, and that led to his fall. Since his fall, of course, he is called Satan, the Devil, the wicked one, that old dragon, and many other names.

In Revelation 12:3–4 we read:

> And there appeared another wonder in heaven; and behold a great red dragon, having seven heads and ten horns, and seven crowns upon his heads. And his tail drew the third part of the stars of heaven, and did cast them to the earth: and the dragon stood before the woman which was ready to be delivered, for to devour her child as soon as it was born.

We know that this event has not actually taken place yet, but it will take place at the mid-point of the Tribulation period. Satan at that time will be cast down to earth. No longer will he have access to the throne of God as he does at this time, as pointed out in Job 1. In verses 7–8 of Revelation 12 we read:

> And there was war in heaven: Michael and his angels fought against the dragon; and the dragon fought and his angels, And prevailed not; neither was their place found any more in heaven.

So, he will lose his access to heavenly places at that time. In verse 9 it says:

> And the great dragon was cast out, that old serpent, called the Devil, and Satan, which deceiveth the whole world: he was cast out into the earth, and his angels were cast out with him.

We speak about war in heaven, but, of course, we know from other scriptures that there has been war in heaven ever since the Devil decided to take over the Kingdom of God; the universe. So, that war has continued, and what we read here in Revelation is the conclusion of that war. There is going to be an even greater war between the angels of God and the fallen angels of Satan. We thereby see the conclusion of this battle that has been going on in the heavens in Revelation 12. We know that he is going about "seeking whom he may devour, and to deceive," because he knows his time is short. That is why we see so much satanic activity in the world today. He knows that his time is growing shorter with each passing day.

What about Satan's fallen angels and other references concerning the traffic and efforts of the Devil to take over this world? We saw in Revelation 12 the identity of the leader of the fallen angels. First, let us look at the angels that are *bound,* which means that they do not have freedom or access of movement, because they are imprisoned at this particular point. We want to see who they are and why they are in prison. Let us turn to 2 Peter 2:4–5, where we read:

> For if God spared not the angels that sinned, but cast them down to hell, and delivered them into chains of darkness, to be reserved unto judgment; And spared not the old world, but saved Noah the eighth person, a preacher of righteousness, bringing in the flood upon the world of the ungodly.

We then see the identity of those who are bound, and when this imprisonment actually took place, which goes back to Genesis 6. These angels that were bound are related to Noah's day, and we read in Genesis 6 that "the sons of God" took unto themselves "the daughters of men."

In Scripture we read that Adam was created a son of

God; he was a son of God by direct creation. He was the first son of God, but he fell and lost that sonship relationship. When you go to Luke, the *next* man who is mentioned being *the* son of God is Jesus Christ. He was a son of God by conception of the Holy Spirit. Between the first Adam and the second Adam you will not find any human being referred to in the Bible as "a son of God," except prophetically. In Hosea we read that in *that day* it shall be said of Israel: "Ye are the sons of the living God." Today, anyone who is not saved is not a son of God. We are sons of God by adoption; sonship was restored only through Jesus Christ.

So the sons of God of Genesis 6 have to be fallen angels, as referred to here in 2 Peter. There are some who say these people were the sons of Seth, and they have their reasons for believing this. But, if we go back and study the main theologians of past centuries—back to Josephus even—Josephus clearly says that they are angels. Josephus was a Jewish priest, so we have to give him credit for at least knowing his own language. The term, "sons of God," in the Hebrew, occurs five times in the Old Testament, one of which is in Genesis 6, and no one will argue that the other four places mean "angels," so why not here, also?

These angels took on themselves the form of men, left their first estate, and other scriptures refer to them "going after strange flesh." There is nothing that tells us that these beings were anything but angels, and we see that God has reserved those angels in chains where they can do no more damage or pervert the human race as they did before the flood. This is their judgment. Other fallen angels await this judgment, but they are free with Satan at this time. The fallen angels which are bound are referred to again in Jude, verses 6–7 where it says:

> And the angels which kept not their first estate, but left their own habitation, he hath reserved in everlasting chains under darkness unto the judgment of the great day. Even as Sodom and Gomorrha, and the cities about them in like manner, giving themselves over to fornication, and going after strange flesh, are set forth for an example, suffering the vengeance of eternal fire.

This must relate back to Genesis because that is the only context in which this can be placed. These verses state that these angels have been taken out of being free; they are chained; they are awaiting their judgment, which is to be cast into the lake of fire.

Turning to 1 Peter 3:19 we read these words by Peter: "By which also he went and preached unto the spirits in prison." This is speaking of Christ during the time He was in the tomb after His crucifixion and before His ascension. We continue reading in 1 Peter 3:20:

> Which sometime were disobedient, when once the longsuffering of God waited in the days of Noah, while the ark was a preparing, wherein few, that is, eight souls were saved by water.

Once again we see this group identified with Genesis 6.

The next group to be considered are the fallen angels who are free. One of the best examples of this, though we see it throughout the entire New Testament, particularly in Christ's ministry, are the demons that were cast out. They would have had to be free in order to be cast out. Probably the best example of this is the demon-possessed maniac of Gadara in Luke 8:26–36. They called themselves Legion, for there were many, and they all took abode in the maniac's body and were living through him and causing untold suffering. Christ, when He saw the man, heard him say: "What have I to do with thee, Jesus. . . . I beseech thee, torment me not." These demons were concerned that it was not their time, when they would be cast into the lake of fire. Christ cast them out of the man, and the demons requested to be cast into a herd of swine. Why the swine were in Israel is not known, but the whole herd ran down a steep slope into the lake and drowned. What happened to the demons? It is not known if they were then freed from the swine, or sent on to await in the darkness their final judgment.

The next scripture we refer to is 1 Timothy 4:1:

> Now the Spirit speaketh expressly, that in the latter times some shall depart from the faith, giving heed to seducing spirits, and doctrines of devils.

If there has ever been a time in the history of Christianity where church members are departing from the faith, it is *today.*

There is today, also, the question of "demon possession." Do we have demon possession as it relates to the time in which we presently live? Are people still being possessed by demons? Can Christians be possessed by demons?

There are different thoughts on this, and many theologians have different ideas regarding demonic activity in the present day. From Christ's message in Matthew about the "strong man," it appears that if the Holy Spirit is indwelling us, then we cannot be possessed by *any other* spirit. Christians today are certainly influenced by demons, but Christians do not have to be controlled by demons. Christians at times are appointed a demon by Satan to be a thorn in the flesh, just as Paul had his thorn in the flesh.

Paul's thorn was possibly a demon who was assigned to torment him. Yes, we believe that demons are active today, because there is no place in Scripture where it is stated that the demon activity was ever removed from mankind. While demons can test Christians, they cannot possess Christians.

Going to Haiti, or even Florida, one can see voodoo activity which is nothing but demon possession. These people who are possessed move and talk as if they are being controlled by a foreign entity. There is no other way that it can be explain. Going into Africa you can see the same thing. You can go into the temples of Thailand and watch the temple dancers who are acting a part. There will be a young girl singing in a high soprano voice, which is indigenous to young Asian girls. This girl, who will accompany herself, or who has an accompanist, sings about those things which the dancers are acting out or portraying. Perhaps they are acting out a snake, or a monkey demon, or some other demon, or perhaps there will be several demon actors on the stage at one time. This girl with the high soprano voice, as she begins singing about the demons, has a complete change in her facial expression, and her voice begins to come from deep inside her and becomes guttural. This is *demon possession.*

Demon possession manifests itself in many ways. It is not known how many in this country are possessed by demons, but it is certainly one of Satan's wiles as referred to in Scripture. The old Devil is at work in many areas today, and that includes demon possession. Christians are born-again and indwelt by the Holy Spirit and cannot be demon possessed, but there are many others who are being possessed by demons, and giving *heed* to alien spirits. These demon, or alien, spirits are certainly influencing the world today.

There are some today who claim that they can cast out demons. This could be a very dangerous thing, because there are those in the New Testament who tried and the demons jumped on them and tore them to pieces. In the first place, the average person would have a difficult time truly identifying someone who is demon possessed. Do Christians have that ability? In this age, since the apostles have gone (and there being no apostolic succession), to help someone who perhaps is demon possessed or demon influenced, is to introduce them to Christ and the Holy Spirit who will enter them and dispossess their body of the demon. This is the Christian's power to cast out demons, which is the giving of the Gospel of Jesus Christ to those with lost souls. It is the Christian's obligation to do this to the glory of God the Father.

We next consider the "types" of angels and the chronology of authority among the angelic host. The different types of angels are represented in Scripture in, more or less, a pyramid of authority. In as far as the fallen angels are concerned, Lucifer would be at the top of that pyramid, and at the pyramid of God's angels would be Michael, or perhaps Gabriel. All of God's creation encompasses the "cosmos," or "the world." This can be understood from Colossians 1:16–17:

> For by him were all things created, that are in heaven, and that are in earth, visible and invisible, whether they be thrones, or dominions, or principalities, or powers: all things were created by him, and for him: And he is before all things, and by him all things consist.

Louis Sperry Chafer, a noted theologian, gives several good definitions of the things referred to in this scripture. "Thrones" refer to "those who sat upon them."

"Dominions" refer to "those who rule." "Principalities" refer to "those who govern." "Powers" refer to "those who exercise supremacy," and "authorities" refer to "those invested with imperial responsibility." Each one of these, whether they follow God or follow Lucifer, have a particular job to do, and it is to be done in order—which means someone is in charge *of them*. God is in charge of His angels; Satan is in charge of the rebel angels.

IV.
Archangels, Watchers, and Holy Ones

Lucifer is the most prominent fallen angel mentioned in Scripture, but what powers does Lucifer really have? Does he do what he wants to do? Is he limited in scope? Just how does God control him? Or, does God have any control over Satan?

First of all, Lucifer was created. He is not omnipresent, which means that he is not present everywhere at one time. He is like a human; both were created. When God created man, man was made subject to limitations. Since he is not omnipresent, Satan must have many ministers looking after his work for him. Looking at Ezekiel 28:13 we can see what God has to say about this:

> •Thou hast been in Eden the garden of God; every precious stone was thy covering, the sardius, topaz, and the diamond, the beryl, the onyx, and the jasper, the sapphire, the emerald, and the carbuncle, and gold: the workmanship of thy tabrets and of thy pipes was prepared in thee in the day that thou was *created* [emphasis added].

There is a saying that was popular several years ago: "The Devil made me do it." That is taking much for granted when any individual would think that he or she has the complete attention of Satan. Only a few humans, such as Adam, Eve, and Job, had that distinction.

But we see in Ephesians 6:11–12 that Satan has many helpers.

> Put on the whole armour of God, that ye may be able to stand against the wiles of the devil. For we wrestle not against flesh and blood, but against principalities, against powers, against the rulers of the darkness of this world, against spiritual wickedness in high places.

Nevertheless, Satan does have limitations. For example, we read in Job 1:12:

> And the LORD said unto Satan, Behold, all that he [Job] hath is in thy power; only upon himself put not forth thine hand. So Satan went forth from the presence of the LORD.

This verse shows that Satan cannot do everything that he wants to do, just those things that God allows him to do. If he could do everything that he wanted to do, then we as Christians would be tormented even worse than Job.

The name "Lucifer" means "the bright and shining one," and that is one of the characteristics of the Devil. While he was Lucifer (he is no longer called Lucifer, of course, because he is Satan and the Devil, enemy of God and man) he was the bright and shining one—which he is no longer—but he takes on this characteristic to deceive according to the apostle Paul.

There is another identification of Satan: he appeared as a serpent; a snake. Fausset says of that:

> A serpent. The form under which Satan, the old serpent, tempted Eve. The serpent being known as subtle, Eve was not surprised at his speaking, and did not suspect a spiritual foe. Its crested head of pride, glittering skin, fascinated, unshaded, gaited eyes, shameless lust, tortuous movement, venomous bite, groveling posture, all adapt it to be types of Satan.

Satan was a serpent, also called seraph, or seraphim. We read of seraphim: "God's attending angels." Seraphim in Isaiah 6:2 means "a flying serpent," or "fiery serpent." Further down we read that it was one of Satan's order. Evidently, Satan, before he fell, was a seraphim, and doubtless a beautiful creature, but after he tempted Eve the serpent was no longer a beautiful creature. This is because God pronounced a curse upon him and said: "Thou are cursed above all cattle, and above every beast of the field . . . upon thy belly shalt thou go, and dust shalt thou eat all the days of your life." God said that men would try to crush his head, and we know that is what Jesus did at the cross. After Satan brought sin, the serpent became a despised, hateful symbol to be feared. Seraphim, though, was the beautiful form of Satan before he sinned.

What is the highest type of angelic host? The highest type of angel, and certainly Satan's equal, is the archangel. Though there are those who believe that there is more than one archangel, it can be seen in Scripture that Michael is the only one named as an archangel. Michael's name means, "Who is like God?" We see Michael in Jude verse 9. Jude is known for several revelations that no one else refers to in Scripture. In this verse it says:

> Yet Michael the archangel, when contending with the devil he disputed about the body of Moses, durst not

bring against him a railing accusation, but said, The Lord rebuke thee.

We may get the idea from this verse that Satan possibly has more power than Michael. It is not known if that is the case, but here it would appear to perhaps infer that. God buried Moses, and after the burial Satan came along and wanted to dig up his body and carry it off. There is no reason given as to why he would want to do this.

It is known that Moses died at the age of 120, and God buried him where no man knew, but we also read that when he died his body was still perfect, his eyesight was still perfect, he was still an excellent physical specimen. Satan evidently desired Moses' body, and he even fought for it. We read also about the two witnesses in Revelation, and we believe that Moses and Elijah will be the two witnesses, the reason being that they were the ones with Christ on the Mount of Transfiguration. Therefore, there is something about the body of Moses that we do not understand. Did he have a resurrection after his death? Did God raise him for a particular mission to be attended to in the future? None of that is known, but there is some reason why the Devil wanted Moses' body.

Although these ideas may present a conclusion, we think there is a modicum of credibility to some of these suggestions. There is even the possibility that had Satan gotten hold of Moses' body, he [Satan] might have entered that body to approach Israel. We can only suggest what the Scriptures might infer, without drawing any definite conclusions.

The next time that Michael the archangel is mentioned is in Daniel 10:13:

But the prince of the kingdom of Persia withstood me

> one and twenty days: but, lo, Michael, one of the chief princes, came to help me; and I remained there with the kings of Persia.

Since Michael is one of the chief princes, we see again there are other chief princes, also. Are there only three distinguishing chief princes, or are there others? The prince of Persia mentioned in this verse is included in the chief princes, and had evidently been assigned to an ungodly nation.

We see Michael again in Daniel 12:1 where he is defending Israel. In Revelation 12:7–12 we see that Michael is the head of God's army. In 1 Thessalonians 4:16. Paul says:

> For the Lord himself shall descend from heaven with a shout, with the voice of the archangel, and with the trump of God: and the dead in Christ shall rise first.

It says here that one of the things Michael will be doing as an archangel will be to come with Christ and precede Him with a shout. This mighty shout will rouse the saints and His bride, the trumpet will sound, and then shall they all be with Him in the air.

As we proceed, the next angel we see is Gabriel. In Daniel 8:16 we see that he is the "hero of God."

The next group of angels we want to look at are mentioned in Daniel 4:17. These are two very unusual types:

> This matter is by the decree of the *watchers,* and the demand by the word of the *holy ones:* to the intent that the living may know that the most High ruleth in the kingdom of men, and giveth it to whomsoever he will,

and setteth up over it the basest of men.

What we have here are two classes of spirit beings, two different categories of angels: watchers and holy ones. Evidently in the decision and judgment to be carried out against the king of Babylon, watchers and holy ones were involved. These are angelic beings in God's holy kingdom.

Turning to Revelation 4:6 we read:

> . . . and round about the throne, were four beasts full of eyes before and behind.

These are watchers.

> And the first beast was like a lion, and the second beast like a calf, and the third beast had a face as a man, and the fourth beast was like a flying eagle (vs. 7).

We proceed to verse 8 where it says:

> And the four beasts had each of them six wings about him [or seraphim]; and they were full of eyes within: and they rest not day and night, saying, Holy, holy, holy, Lord God Almighty. . . .

Going on down to verse 10 we read:

> The four and twenty elders fall down before him that sat on the throne, and worship him that liveth for ever and ever. . . .

Here again we see the watchers and the elders (or holy ones) mentioned together just as they are in the book of Daniel. Evidently there are four watchers that God has established to be over His Creation.

God has created everything, and it is His will that everything produce after its own kind. We look at creation today and how it is sustained—how salmon swim upstream to spawn, giant turtles come upon the beaches once a year to lay eggs, and the magic of life in the reproduction of life with the variety of life. Amazing! Astounding! So, according to Scripture, God has watchers over different categories: the beasts of the field; domestic animals; the wild animals; the birds; mankind. That is the mission of the watchers; that is why they were created. It is the same with the elders and holy ones. We read in one verse that there are twenty-four of them. Some say that they represent twelve apostles and twelve of the Old Testament patriarchs, but that is a conclusion. We do not know who these elders are except they must be from the heavenly host that God has ordained. We see that they sat upon seats, or thrones. When someone runs for Congress, they run for a seat—a seat of delegated authority. This, then, is the mission of the holy ones, or the four and twenty elders. The watchers are evidently seraphim, just as Lucifer was a seraphim.

We read in Habakkuk 1:14 these words:

> And makest men as the fishes of the sea, as the creeping things, that have no ruler over them?

This must be the serpent kingdom and the reptile kingdom. We know that dinosaurs were reptiles—reptilian form—and so was Satan. The creeping things have no king over them. Was this because the chief seraph, Satan, fell? Was Satan one of the watchers, and numbered among the watchers and seraphim? It is very possible that this is what happened. We feel that somehow the demise of the dinosaur is associated with Lucifer's rebellion and fall.

Whether this happened before Satan deceived Adam and Eve to sin, or after, is not known. But no one has ever been able to explain what happened to the dinosaurs.

V.

Guardian Angels

As we have noted previously, seraphim are mentioned in the Bible in several places, and they are one of the orders of angels. "Seraphim" is actually a root word for "serpent," and we read that Satan came into the Garden of Eden in the form of a serpent. Evidently, at one time, a serpent was not something to be feared. Scripture actually indicates that Satan was a very beautiful angel, "the light bearer," but after he beguiled Adam and Eve to sin, then the serpent became an ugly, despicable form of life. God said that the serpent would crawl on its belly in the dust and would be ground under the heel of men.

It seems that most people are born with an innate fear of the serpent, or the snake. It also seems that man is going to great trouble today to try to help us get over the fear of serpents. It is not known whether there is an ulterior motive involved in that or not, but there are even programs on television where it is shown that the serpent is really just another animal; there is nothing to fear and we have a lot to gain from it, even to the point that many children are taken to zoos where they can handle the serpents. This builds up a callousness toward the fear of the serpent. Man has been, at least psychologically, prepared not to fear Satan in this day and age. Man is being programmed to accept many fearful beings mentioned by Jesus.

The cherubim is also another very important spirit

being. The first time that we read about cherubim is in Genesis 3:24. We find them guarding the throne of God. In this particular scene, they are guarding the entrance to the Garden of Eden:

> So he drove out the man; and he placed at the east of the garden of Eden Cherubims, and a flaming sword which turned every way, to keep the way of the tree of life.

God has placed these formidable looking beings to keep man, especially Adam and Eve, from re-entering the Garden and eating of the Tree of Life. We know that the Tree of Life, according to the book of Revelation, is today in heaven, and will be part of the New Heaven and New Earth.

We see cherubim again in Exodus 25:18–19 where we read:

> And thou shalt make two cherubims of gold, of beaten work shalt thou make them, in the two ends of the mercy seat. And make one cherub on the one end, and the other cherub on the other end: even of the mercy seat shall ye make the cherubims on the two ends thereof.

In Revelation, although cherubim are not mentioned by name, we see them as guardian angels of God keeping watch over the universe. We know that the universe is the kingdom of God, and the ruler over a kingdom needs different kinds of officers, soldiers, or administrators. Therefore, God has different orders of angels, and seraphim and cherubim are two of the orders of angels. We read in Ezekiel 10:13–15, these words:

> As for the wheels, it was cried unto them in my hearing, O wheel. And every one had four faces: the first face was the face of a cherub, and the second face was the face of a man, and the third the face of a lion, and the fourth the face of an eagle. And the cherubims were lifted up. This is the living creature that I saw by the river of Chebar.

We read in Revelation about the watchers. The watchers are also cherubim, or God's guardians over the creation.

There are other types of angels referred to in the Bible such as the "elect" angels. This is an unusual grouping of angels, so what does Scripture have to say about these "elect" angels?

The only place that the elect angels are mentioned is 1 Timothy 5:21 where Paul states:

> I charge thee before God, and the Lord Jesus Christ, and the elect angels, that thou observe these things without preferring one before another, doing nothing by partiality.

It is not certain if this is simply a reference to those angels who have followed God, or this is a specific group of angels. He gives them a specific task, and this specific task is so general that it could be given to all angels. The elect angels are probably the ones who decided to follow Him. We will meet these angels in heaven around the throne of God. The elect angels are evidently those who elected by their own volition to not follow Satan in his rebellion. It is interesting that even the angels have a free moral choice. They still have their freedom of choice, just as man has a free choice to accept or reject the Lord Jesus Christ. The elect angels shouted for joy at the birth of Jesus Christ.

The elect angels are those who administer in God's Kingdom.

What is there to know about guardian angels? Although there is some information about guardian angels in the Bible, there are mistaken ideas about guardian angels. Many people try to build a case for guardian angels out of the verse in Matthew 4:6, and again in 18:10. Does every individual have a guardian angel, or just specific ones who are assigned by God? Certainly there are enough angels to go around, but does God just give them direction as He sees fit? In Matthew 4:6 we read:

> And [Satan] saith unto him, If thou be the Son of God, cast thyself down: for it is written, He shall give his angels charge concerning thee. . . .

Many people use this verse to claim that all Christians have guardian angels. Then, looking over in Matthew 18:10, we read:

> Take heed that ye despise not one of these little ones; for I say unto you, That in heaven their angels do always behold the face of my Father which is in heaven.

There are those who say that this means that every child is appointed an angel to look after them, but it would seem that these angels beholding the face of God are just awaiting directions; awaiting orders on what to do. There are so many things that are happening to children in the world today, and if they all have guardian angels, then their guardian angels are asleep, or just not paying attention. It is believed that, at times, there is angelic intervention in the lives of children, and in the lives of Christians, but this does not mean that every child who is born in the world has a guardian angel until he reaches the age of accountability.

For example, look what happened to the children in the Holocaust. Over a million Jewish children were killed in the Holocaust. If these children had guardian angels over them, then what were they doing when these children were mutilated and died such horrible deaths in the gas chambers? What about the children in the United States who are being molested, raped, and abused? What about those children in Africa who are dying of starvation? We know that there is angelic intervention by assignment, and there may be angelic intervention in your life by assignment. If a person is in the will of God and has an important work to do for God, and it is to God's glory that that person continue in service, then certainly there is no disputing angelic intervention.

In a recent issue of *Field and Stream,* which is not a religious publication, an unusual case was presented. A 6-year-old child who was out playing by himself was bitten by a large rattlesnake. The snake had so much venom that the bite immediately rendered the child helpless, and he later could not even remember what took place. People said it was miraculous that he even lived. When the boy was taken to the hospital he could not talk, thus he could not relate to them what had happened. After much pain and deterioration in his body, he began to recover and he was asked: "Son, how did you get home?" The child related the story that a man in a white coat picked him up, carried him home, and placed him on his doorstep. If that is a true case—and the boy had no reason to lie—then we would believe that this was divine intervention by God who gave one of His angels direction to help this child.

Much is heard today of individuals relating stories of how an angel came to the foot of their bed during the night and relayed to them in detail prophetic events yet to take place. Most of the time we do not hear about these revelations until after the prophetic "events" have taken place. Some people today believe that they have received visions, or dreams, from God, but there is no place in Scripture that shows that God works in dreams and visions anymore. He has given us His completed Word and there is no need for added revelation. So, the guardian angels, if indeed they are active in this age (and we know they do exist in particular cases), are not the norm, but are instead the exception.

As mentioned before, it is believed that there is angelic intervention, or protection, but it is by special assignment, or special mission. Let's go back to the young lad who was bitten by this huge snake. There are some rattlesnakes in the Florida swamps that get as large as ten to twelve feet long. Diamondback rattlers do not get that big anywhere else, but they do grow that large in Florida. That was the type of rattlesnake that bit the boy. In the hospital the boy was put on a respirator, and his body swelled up so huge that they had to split his skin to prevent his body from bursting, yet he lived. While recovering he then related the story of the man in the white coat carrying him home. There was no other explanation as to how he could have gotten home. Who knows what mission God has for this young boy in the future.

One final word on guardian angels. There are many places in Scripture where they are described as intervening. Daniel in the lion's den is one example, where the Lord sent the angels to shut the mouths of the lions. There are many examples in Scripture of angelic intervention in the lives of saints, or even in the lives of children. But, as far as everyone having a guardian angel, or every child having a guardian angel, that is difficult to substantiate in Scripture.

What about the angel of the Lord? There are several scriptures about the angel of the Lord. Is there only one angel of the Lord? Who is the angel of the Lord which is referred to in Scripture? The angel of the Lord appears several times in the Old Testament where the phrase actually means—in the Hebrew—either one of two things: "Theophany," which is God manifested in the flesh, or "Christophany," which is Christ manifested in the flesh. One of those places that is referred to is Genesis 18:1–2:

> And the Lord appeared unto him in the plains of Mamre: and he sat in the tent door in the heat of the day; And he lift up his eyes and looked, and, lo, three men stood by him: and when he saw them, he ran to meet them from the tent door, and bowed himself toward the ground.

This is a case of Abraham being visited by the Lord and two other angels. He appeared to Joshua in Joshua 5:13, and he appeared to Samson's parents in Judges 13:3. So, the angel of the Lord appears many times in the Old Testament. This was not just a messenger of God, but God Himself manifested in the flesh. It was the Messiah appearing to the Old Testament saints as in the case of Abraham, Daniel, Moses, and others. Jesus Christ is "I Am," the One Who created all things, and for Whom all things were created. Therefore, He made preincarnate appearances to the Old Testament saints before He came and tabernacled among men in the flesh.

VI.
Angels in the Old Testament

As you go from Genesis to Revelation using a concordance to trace the ministry of angels both in the Old and New Testaments, it is amazing to see the number of times that angels intervene in the testimony and service of the prophets, and even of the apostles and members of the early New Testament church. In this chapter we will resume the study of angels in the Old Testament.

The second time that angels are mentioned in the Old Testament is in Genesis 6, beginning in verse 1:

> And it came to pass, when men began to multiply on the face of the earth, and daughters were born unto them, That the sons of God saw the daughters of men that they were fair; and they took them wives of all which they chose.

There is disagreement among theologians and some Bible teachers as to whether these beings were actually angels or not. However, the weight of evidence shows that these were indeed angels. Most theologians have a very definite belief about this, but let us go back and look at some of the traditional views of men that are considered to be reliable. As noted before, there is a controversy among theologians, authors, ministers, and pastors, about whether the sons of God of Genesis 6 were the descendants of Seth, or were angelic beings. Matthew Henry and the Scofield Bible interprets them to be sons of Seth, *not* angels. Josephus had much to say about Genesis 6, and he must at least be given credit for knowing his own language, which was Hebrew. Let us see, then, what Josephus had to say. He wrote:

> Many angels of God accompanied with women and begat sons that proved unjust and despisers of all that was good on account of their own strength. These men did what resembled the acts of those whom the Grecians called giants. There was still then left a race of giants who had bodies so large and countenance so entirely different from other men, that they were surprising to the sight and terrible to the hearing. The bones of these men are still shown to this very day.

Josephus, as mentioned before, was commissioned by the Roman government to write *The Wars of the Jews,* and Josephus, in fear of his own head, would not have written something that could not at least have been substantiated in his day. Evidently, the bones of the giants were still very much in evidence in the days of Josephus; the time of Christ. But Josephus said without reservations or qualifications that the sons of God in Genesis 6:2 were angels. They are also referred to in the New Testament in 2 Peter, and also in Jude. In 2 Peter 2: 4–5 we read:

> For if God spared not the angels that sinned, but cast them down to hell, and delivered them into chains of darkness, to be reserved unto judgment; And spared not the old world, but saved Noah. . . .

So here, the angels that God cast down to the earth are associated with the flood and the days of Noah. Also there are references in the book of Jude, and many other references, which tie the angels who left their first estate and followed after Satan, to those angels who took upon themselves the sexual properties of men and cohabited with women.

It is very interesting that Josephus would say that the bones of these men were still shown to this very day. What has happened to them? They were here nineteen hundred years ago. There are some who think that the footprints in the Paluxy River near Glen Rose, Texas—some of these prints are eighteen to twenty-two inches long—found in the rock-bed along with dinosaur footprints, are prints of giants. If these are footprints of giants, then certainly this would bear Moses and Josephus out.

But, the subject of "the sons of God" is something that many theologians and scholars become very passionate about. Who are "the sons of God"? From whence did they come? The sons of God, the angels, were a direct creation of God, but why would God allow a creature to sin? We may not understand this because God's ways are higher than our ways. How could Lucifer, uninfluenced, commit sin on his own? How could Lucifer think he could replace God? As to Genesis 6, it would seem that the weight of the proof is in the text itself.

What is the major objection to the "angels of God" theory? One of the objections is the statement by Jesus that in the resurrection we will be as the angels of God in heaven who neither marry nor are given in marriage, but the qualification here is "the angels of God in heaven." He made no references to the angels who "kept not their first estate" and followed Satan, who are known as the angels of Satan. The Bible speaks of the "angels of Satan" and the "angels of God." The angels of Satan are those who, according to Scripture, left their created order—their first estate—and took on a lifestyle like unto man in order to marry with the women of earth. Martin Luther believed that they were angels; he taught that. We also read from *Dake's Annotated Reference Bible:*

> There are two classes of fallen angels. Those with Satan who will be cast down to earth during the future Tribulation, and those who are now down in hell for committing fornication.

Dake's Annotated Bible goes on to say that those who committed fornication were those before the flood who cohabited with women.

Clarence Larkin is another well-known scholar, and he says:

> If the sons of Seth and the daughters of Cain were men, why did not Moses, who wrote the Pentateuch, say so. Is it not sufficient to say the men in Moses time knew what he meant?

Clarence Larkin goes on to use terminology in the Old Testament, and brings out quite explicitly, that Genesis 6 means angels. The Pilgrim Bible also interprets them to be angels. It would be possible to quote source after source. For instance, the Companion Bible clearly brings out from the original Hebrew that the sons of God of Genesis 6 were angels who left their first estate, their created order, and cohabited with women.

Continuing on from Genesis 6, what about the angels that visited Abraham? In Genesis 18:1–3 we read of this occurrence:

And the LORD appeared unto him [speaking of Abraham] in the plains of Mamre: and he sat in the tent door in the heat of the day; And he lift up his eyes and looked, and, lo, three men stood by him: and when he saw them, he ran to meet them from the tent door, and bowed himself toward the ground, And said, My Lord, if now I have found favour in thy sight, pass not away, I pray thee, from thy servant.

Evidently, Abraham immediately recognized who this person was. We are speaking of "the angel of the Lord" here, Christ appearing in the Old Testament.

This brings us to a very interesting thought. In Psalm 8:5 we read that man was made "a little lower than the angels"—a little less in power, perhaps a little less in stature, but certainly not as powerful as the angels. Then in Matthew and Luke where the Lord Jesus Christ is born and comes upon the scene, it is said that He is made in the image of God. There are those who propose that the Creator, Jesus Christ who created all things, fashioned His body prior to the creation. Then the Word says that man was made in their image, so there are those who believe—Henry Morris is one of these—that Adam and the rest of the race were created after the pattern that already existed in Jesus Christ. Then when He came, His image was what had been created prior to that. Now we see that the angels appear with Christ to Abraham, and he recognizes them immediately. So, throughout the Old Testament it can be seen that angels appear in the form of a man, and they are instantly recognizable.

As the chapter continues Abraham has a calf killed, he feeds them, they eat, and after that the angel of the Lord goes on to say that one of the reasons that He came was to destroy Sodom and Gomorrah. Abraham immediately protests because his nephew, Lot, is in Sodom. We read in Genesis to 19:1:

> And there came two angels to Sodom at even; and Lot sat in the gate of Sodom: and Lot seeing them rose up to meet them; and he bowed himself with his face toward the ground.

The text of Genesis 18:24 indicates that Abraham began by asking if there were fifty righteous souls could not the city be spared, and works his way down to ten righteous souls. Verse 34 of that chapter tells us that there were not even ten righteous souls in Sodom. The population of that city is not known, but a moral parallel can be drawn from that concerning the United States. The U.S. has dropped to the lowest level it has ever been spiritually, and were it not for a few righteous persons, God would certainly rain down His judgment on this country.

The Bible tells of the judgments coming upon the world during the Tribulation, and God would not bring such judgments on the world as long as His children were in the world. This is why the authors believe that His Church is going to be Raptured before the Tribulation period begins. At least that is one of the reasons. God did not bring judgment on Sodom and Gomorrah until after Lot and his family had departed. We don't believe that the Scriptures teach that God will bring judgment upon the world and the Tribulation until the Church—God's children—are taken out of the world.

It is to be noted that angels have power to do things like destroy, fight, cause men to be blinded. Evidently angels have power that ordinary men do not have. One of the interesting things about angels is that they can appear and disappear at will. Some people say about UFO's, that they were the only one who saw it, but there are incidents where several people have said that they saw the same UFO. This is not proposing that everyone who sees a UFO, or reports seeing something that they can't identify, has seen an angel from heaven. However, the possibility exists, because we know that angels can appear and disappear.

While growing up in Hugo, which is in southeast Oklahoma, I saw three unidentified flying objects streaking across the sky. When they were right over me they stopped and just remained motionless. It was a little after sundown, so I sat down and watched the objects for an hour until it got completely dark. These stationary objects were blinking white, blue, and orange. I went into the house to eat dinner, but when I came out again, the objects were gone. At that particular time no one had heard of a UFO, and I had no idea what it was I had seen in the sky. Yet, what I saw was not something made here on earth, nor could they have been controlled by any human being. There is no way that a man could have withstood the centrifugal force under which these things operated. I believe in UFO's as being angelic intervention. Whether they are satanic, or angels of God, or chariots of God, is something that is not known. Many believe that they are demons or angels of Satan.

In any event, it is known that angels materialize and then disappear. One of the most interesting occurrences happened to Elisha when Syria was advancing against Israel in 2 Kings 6. A young man had come to Elisha to tell him that he didn't see how in the world they were going to be able to overcome the enemy, because they were so badly outnumbered. Verse 16 gives the answer:

And he answered, Fear not: for they that be with us are

more than they that be with them [speaking of the enemy, Syria].

This young man was quite unnerved because he didn't understand, nor could he see the angels. Verse 17 says:

> And Elisha prayed, and said, LORD, I pray thee, open his eyes, that he may see. And the LORD opened the eyes of the young man; and he saw: and, behold, the mountain was full of horses and chariots of fire round about Elisha.

The young man saw that they were not by themselves, and that there were more angels than there was enemy. This is a very good example of how the angels appear or disappear. Today we hear of people who claim that an angel stood at the foot of their bed and explained how God was going to perform certain things. These people claim they were not afraid, but were instead very comfortable. There are some problems with this, because in most instances in Scripture when an angel appeared to someone, they were very afraid. It is not a natural thing for us to see a supernatural being. We see in this particular case, however, that the angels were there all of the time, but the young man could not see them. Elisha, however, knew that they were there.

There are many other instances in the Old Testament to cite, like the illustration of Jacob's ladder in Genesis 28:12, and "the angels of God ascending and descending on it"; the appearance of one who "is like the Son of God" with Shadrach, Meshach, and Abednego in the fiery furnace; the angels who shut the mouths of the lions, as referred to in Daniel 6:22, to save God's prophet from being devoured by the animals. Example after example could be cited from the Old Testament regarding the appearance and ministry of angels.

VII.

Angels in the New Testament

Thus far we have confined our study of angels mainly to their presence and ministry in the Old Testament. Now we study the ministry of angels in the New Testament.

When angels are introduced to us in the Gospels, they are associated with the birth, ministry, death, and resurrection of Jesus Christ. Paul wrote in 1 Timothy 3:16 that Christ was "seen of angels," meaning they were with Him continuously in everything He did from His birth announcement until His ascension. The angels were at His beck and call. Christ said in Matthew 26:53 that He could call legions of angels and they would take care of the situation at hand, but He came for another purpose, which was to be born a man, and to die as a man, though He was perfect in every way and knew no sin. These angels were there to accompany Him in all things. Why? Because He was the Son of God, and it is stated in Hebrews that He placed Himself a little lower than the angels. He gave up His royal position, and restrained His own power that He might be able to die for our sins.

Angels appear in the announcement of Jesus' birth in Matthew 1:20:

But while he thought on these things, behold, the angel

of the Lord appeared unto him in a dream, saying, Joseph, thou son of David, fear not to take unto thee Mary thy wife: for that which is conceived in her is of the Holy Ghost.

Here it is seen that angels are mentioned as a part of Christ's ministry in the announcement of His birth. From that point on He was never by Himself; He was always accompanied by these appointed angels. Only His restraining power would keep these angels from doing for Christ what they were created to do—protect Him. The angel in Matthew chapter 1 announced the birth of Jesus, explained how this was going to take place by conception of the Holy Spirit, and exactly when the Child was to be born.

Moving on to Luke 1:11, an angel also announced to Zacharias another birth.

And there appeared unto him an angel of the Lord standing on the right side of the altar of incense.

Twice a year, or every six months, Zacharias was called to fulfill his priestly requirements in the Temple. For four hundred years, since the end of Malachi, God had not directly communicated with man. This is called the "four hundred silent years," because God was silent. For the first time in four hundred years an angel came to speak to man, Zacharias, and he is told that he is to have a child. This child, as it will turn out, is going to be John the Baptist. So, an angel announced the birth of Christ, and the birth of John the Baptist.

Moving on in the ministry of Christ, we see in Matthew 2:13 that an angel came to Joseph and told him that he must "flee into Egypt" to escape the persecution and death of the Christ-child. Then in Matthew 4:11 we read that the angels ministered unto Jesus in the wilderness after Satan had left Him. The angels had been there with Him during this whole period of temptation by the Devil, watching over Him according to 1 Timothy 3:16, but His restraint kept them from intervening. In Matthew 26:53 they were present with Christ in the garden. It is inferred that angels were at the cross because Christ said that He could call down more than twelve legions of His angels to intervene, but He *did not*. Why? Because of His love for all mankind.

We see that an angel was also at Christ's resurrection in Matthew 28. In verse 2 Matthew tells us:

> And, behold, there was a great earthquake: for the angel of the Lord descended from heaven, and came and rolled back the stone from the door, and sat upon it.

The angel at the tomb came to announce to those who came to anoint Christ's body, that He was not there. In Matthew 28:5–6 we read:

> And the angel answered and said unto the women, Fear not ye: for I know that ye seek Jesus, which was crucified. He is not here: for he is risen, as he said. Come, see the place where the Lord lay [past tense— the Lord is no longer there].

Then, in Acts 1:10–11, angels are involved in Christ's ascension:

> And while they looked stedfastly toward heaven as he went up, behold, two men stood by them in white apparel; Which also said, Ye men of Galilee, why stand ye gazing up into heaven? this same Jesus, which is taken

up from you into heaven, shall so come in like manner as ye have seen him go into heaven.

It can be seen once again that from Christ's announcement of His birth to His ascension, that the angels were there proclaiming both what He was doing and what He had done. The angels informed the disciples that He would come back. They gave the onlookers a message—a prophetic message—that this same Jesus that they had seen go, would surely come again "in like manner."

Matthew 18:10 has already been noted where Jesus spoke of the guardian angels of little children. Of course, the word "guardian" is not in the text. The verse just says "their angels," meaning little children's angels. Does this mean that every child has a guardian angel to look after them and protect them? No, that is not what it means, because, as we have already pointed out, many little children are killed in car wrecks, they are abused, they are sexually molested, they die in all kinds of manners just like adults. So, guardian angels are not to protect every child. It is not stated in Scripture that every child has an angel following him around twenty-four hours a day. All that can be said is to refer to what Jesus says here.

There are, certainly, angels by appointment, and there are certain times that angels do appear and protect when it is for the will and purpose of God—His sovereign will. In Luke 16:22–23, is the story of Lazarus and the rich man, and it reads:

And it came to pass, that the beggar died, and was carried by the angels into Abraham's bosom: the rich man also died, and was buried; And in hell he lift up his eyes, being in torments, and seeth Abraham afar off, and Lazarus in his bosom.

The School of Theology at Jerusalem, according to Josephus, taught the Jewish understanding of the ministry of angels in reference to the souls of those who had died. This was a common teaching in Israel. The Jews called Hades "Abraham's bosom"; the Gentiles called it "Paradise." *Paradise* is a Persian word which means "a park, a beautiful place, a place of rest," and that's what Abraham's bosom was: a resting place of those who were saved according to their faith in the Old Testament, and who were waiting there for the Messiah to come and die for their sins. According to this scripture—and Jesus certainly would not have used something that was untrue to illustrate a spiritual truth—the angels carried Lazarus to Abraham's bosom, which was one compartment of Hades. The other compartment was hell, a place of torment.

According to Josephus, Jewish theology taught that the angels also carried the unsaved into hell, and kept them in hell in torment. This is, of course, hard to substantiate by Scripture other than what we read here in Luke 16. After Christ's resurrection we then read that Paradise was taken to heaven in the presence of God. To be absent from the body is to be present with the Lord. In Acts 5:19 we read that there was an angel who opened the prison doors. Are there angels who are doing that today? Perhaps so. We have seen many miracles on our mission trips. There is no way to explain some things that happen except that they occurred by the power of God. Whether angels are taking care of these things is not known. They could be there, but invisible to the human eye. They opened the prison doors for Peter, and they also appeared to Cornelius to prepare him for Peter's visit to explain the Gospel to him.

In Acts 12:7 Peter was delivered from prison by the

angels, and in Acts 12:23 an angel smote Herod because "he gave not God the glory." Herod then died of some kind of affliction, "and he was eaten of worms." Here is an instance where it can be seen that angels carry out the judgments of God by direct appointment. After the Gospels and Acts 13, the New Testament ministry of angels is limited to direct appointments. In other words, they are sent by God at specific times to do specific things.

VIII.

Angels and the Church

In this chapter we are going to study particularly the ministry of angels today. Are angels watching over us? Do they intercede for us in our witness? Do they instruct us? Are angels ministering spirits to us today? Do angels instruct us in prophetic signs? How do angels minister to individual Christians today, or to the Church witness as a whole?

Guardian angels have been mentioned previously at some length, but there are some additional things which we should discuss. Do we have angels who guard us, to take care of us, who watch over us, who keep us from having accidents, or keep us from being attacked? If there are guardian angels, how do they guard us?

Looking at the ministry of angels during the Church Age and turning to the epistles which are written specifically to the Church, we find that angels are actually mentioned very little. In Acts 27 we read of one such incident. The ship which carried Paul to Rome was wrecked, and all on board were afraid for their lives. We read of Paul's response to their fear in verses 21–25:

> But after long abstinence Paul stood forth in the midst of them, and said, Sirs, ye should have hearkened unto me, and not have loosed from Crete, and to have gained this harm and loss. And now I exhort you to be of

good cheer: for there shall be no loss of any man's life among you, but of the ship. For there stood by me this night the angel of God, whose I am, and whom I serve, Saying, Fear not, Paul; thou must be brought before Caesar: and, lo, God hath given thee all them that sail with thee. Wherefore, sirs, be of good cheer: for I believe God, that it shall be even as it was told me.

After that time, though, in the epistles we find angels mentioned quite sparingly. In Romans 8:38 Paul stated: "I am persuaded" that nothing on heaven or earth, even angels, can separate us from the love of God. We know that the angels of God would not intentionally try to separate us from the love of God, but the angels of the Devil would. However, even the angels of the Devil cannot separate us from the love of God.

In 1 Corinthians 13:1 we read: "Though I speak with the tongues . . . of angels," or the language of angels. Some interpret this to mean that we can speak with the language of the angels; in other words, unknown tongues. This is not what is meant. Paul said, "If it were possible to speak with the language of angels." We do not know what language angels speak. Evidently there is a heavenly language. They may not speak Greek, Tagalog, Spanish, German, or English; it would be only a guess that if they spoke any known language, it would be Hebrew. Evidently there is a universal heavenly language that all Christians are going to speak when they get to heaven.

Paul indicates in 1 Corinthians 4:9 in reference to his own persecution—being beaten, humiliated, thrown in the pit with the lions, made a fool, mocked, and laughed at—he said: ". . . we are made a spectacle unto . . . angels." We have an obligation, even to the angels, to conduct ourselves in an acceptable way in persecution and in our walk before the world. Even the angels take note of what we do in reference to being strong in the faith. We read also in Galatians 1:8 this warning: "But though we, or an angel from heaven, preach any other gospel. . . ." We do not know that angels would try to preach another gospel. Certainly the angels of the Devil might influence ministers who are under his authority to preach another gospel, but even if an angel would try to instruct us to preach another gospel, we are not to do it.

In Colossians 2:18 we are again instructed that we are not to worship angels. Although the Bible has much to say about angels and their ministry (there are literally hundreds and hundreds of scriptures in reference to the ministry of angels both in the Old Testament and the New Testament) we are not to be deceived into worshipping angels, or into believing that angels are coming to bring us the latest word from God. Some cults contend that an angel came and showed them where some latest words from God were to be found. The Bible says we are not to believe that "revelation"; that is another gospel. We are warned against that. There are some churches and cults around today who would try to lead us into that error. Paul here says no, you are not to do that; you are not to pay any attention to that because it is a false, satanic gospel. We read warnings in the New Testament about letting angels deceive us, because they are probably angels of the Devil; fallen angels; angels that the Devil is using.

In the gospels when the Kingdom was being offered by Jesus, the ministry of angels was very prevalent. In Matthew, Mark, and Luke, the ministry of angels, or the reference to angels, is mentioned over and over. That was when Jesus Christ was still offering the Kingdom: "Repent, for the kingdom of heaven is at hand." But when we get to the Gospel of John, which was written in A.D. 90, and interpreted the ministry of Christ to the Church, angels are only mentioned four times. In the first twelve chapters of Acts, when the Kingdom was still being offered, angels are mentioned over and over. But, after the twelfth chapter of Acts, the ministry of angels is only mentioned two or three times; in Romans, only once; in Corinthians, only four times (in reference that we should not let angels influence us; the reference here may be to fallen angels). In Galatians angels are mentioned only three or four times and, again, it is not to let an angel even from heaven influence us or deter us from being faithful to the cross of Christ, and His atonement, His sacrifice, shedding His blood for the remission of sins. In 2 Corinthians angels are mentioned only once.

It can be seen that the ministry of angels is mentioned sparingly in the epistles. What are we to understand from this? We are to understand that we are now indwelt by the Holy Spirit, we are saved through grace, and the ministry of angels is in abeyance until the Second Coming of Christ. This does not mean that on special assignments there is not angelic ministering or intervention, but we are not to look to angels today for protection, or for special dispensations toward us. It is just not in the Scripture.

Mentioned earlier was Colossians 2:18 where we are not to worship angels. Paul goes on to talk about this in Romans 1, where he gives a dissertation on the Creator–creature distinction, and exactly how this works. We are told in so many words in Romans chapter 1 that we are not to worship anything that has been created, whether it be an angel, or a four-footed beast. We are to worship only the Creator. There are people around the world who bow down and worship things that they have created themselves, whether it is an image in stone, an image in wood, an image in their own mind, or another person.

These are all created things. The only thing that is not created is God, and Paul says that we are to worship *Him,* and Him alone. It stands to reason that if I can carve something out of stone I must be greater than it; therefore, why should I bow down to something I have created? It should be bowing down to me.

Going on, we see that there are ministering spirits, as mentioned in Hebrews 1:14. In verses 13 and 14 we read:

> But to which of the angels said he at any time, Sit on my right hand, until I make thine enemies thy footstool? Are they not all ministering spirits, sent forth to minister for them who shall be heirs of salvation?

The subject of the text here is Jesus, the Christ, the One Who has been appointed the position of sitting at the right hand of God. This is not a proof text that every person who is to be saved has a guardian angel. It simply means that these ministering spirits are there; they go out on assignment. We see how God works in specific cases in the New Testament in sending angels to do a specific things. This in no way proves that these ministering spirits are guardian angels or that every person has a ministering spirit. Certainly God can do as He pleases with these ministering spirits. In the New Testament, those who are born-again believers in Jesus Christ are indwelt by the Holy Spirit. He is our Helpmeet, and He is the One we are to lean on. We are not to look to other aid, but to Him. This is not to say that God cannot send an angel to intervene in our behalf, or even to help us, but that in no way proves proves angelic protection entitlement.

In Paul's charge to Timothy he told Timothy about administering to the Church, about overseers of the Church, about selective overseers of the Church, and about his duties and responsibilities as a minister of God in the

Church. In charging Timothy he also instructed him that this charge was made before the elect angels. In 1 Peter 1:12 we find that angels even desire to look into the affairs of men.

We know that the Church Age will end with the Rapture of the Church. In Acts 15 we are told that God, in this age, is calling out of the Gentiles "a people for his name. . . . After this I will return, and will build again the tabernacle of David" (vss. 14, 16). The Church Age is going to end with the Rapture of the Church. Is there going to be angelic intervention or assignment at the Rapture of the Church? Very definitely. First Thessalonians 4:13–18 reads:

> But I would not have you to be ignorant, brethren, concerning them which are asleep, that ye sorrow not, even as others which have no hope. For if we believe that Jesus died and rose again, even so them also which sleep in Jesus will God bring with him. For this we say unto you by the word of the Lord, that we which are alive and remain unto the coming of the Lord shall not prevent them which are asleep. For the Lord himself shall descend from heaven with a shout, with the voice of the archangel, and with the trump of God: and the dead in Christ shall rise first: Then we which are alive and remain shall be caught up together with them in the clouds, to meet the Lord in the air: and so shall we ever be with the Lord. Wherefore comfort one another with these words.

The scripture says here, "the voice of the archangel." Who is the archangel? The archangel is Michael, and Michael will definitely come back with Christ, and the voice of the archangel, which we will hear, calls us to resurrection.

IX.

Angels at the Rapture

We will continue this study where the last chapter left off, and that is with the Rapture. Some protest that the Rapture is not mentioned in the Bible. But "Bible" is not mentioned in the Bible. "Rapture" simply means being caught away in a state of joy and happiness, as a bridegroom catches his bride away on the wedding day. What we are talking about here is the resurrection and translation of the Church. Regardless of what it is called, "being caught away," "translation," "Rapture," any word or descriptive phrase would suffice. The translation of the Church is more comprehensibly described in 1 Thessalonians 4, although it is mentioned in other scriptures in the Bible. Each chapter in 1 Thessalonians and 2 Thessalonians ends with a hope or a looking forward to the Second Coming of Christ. Chapter four ends with a description of the translation of the Church. We read in 1 Thessalonians 4, beginning at verse 13:

> But I would not have you to be ignorant, brethren [and there are a lot of people today who are ignorant about the translation of the Church], concerning them which are asleep, that ye sorrow not, even as others which have no hope. For if we believe that Jesus died and rose again, even so them which also sleep in Jesus will God bring with him. [This verse stresses the impor-

tance of the resurrection of Jesus Christ. As Dr. Bob Jones used to say: "If you don't get Jesus up out of the grave, it don't mean nothin." We have to believe that Jesus Christ, the Son of God, died for our sins, was buried, and rose again on the third day, and that He is coming back. This is an essential to faith.] For this we say unto you by the word of the Lord, that we which are alive and remain unto the coming of the Lord shall not prevent [or precede] them which are asleep. [This is a message of particular importance to those who are alive at the coming of the Lord at the end of the age. This is not the second part of the coming of the Lord, this is the first part, when He is coming for the Church. The second time he comes to Israel, literally.] For the Lord himself shall descend from heaven with a shout, with the voice of the archangel, and with the trump of God: and the dead in Christ shall rise first: Then we which are alive and remain shall be caught up together with them in the clouds, to meet the Lord in the air: and so shall we ever be with the Lord. Wherefore comfort one another with these words (vss. 13–18).

At the Rapture, Christians alive at the time will be caught up together with those who are raised from the dead. In other words, all those who are alive are going to be changed immediately into a glorified body, and then meet up with those Christians who have been dead; those who sleep in Jesus. They, too, will be in their glorified bodies and we will be caught up together in the clouds, and we will meet the Lord in the air.

What about the word "clouds"? There seems to be some controversy or misunderstanding about the word "clouds" used here. There are two words in the original Greek for clouds. One of the two words is found in

Hebrews 12:1 which is *nethos,* and it is simply a cloudy, shapeless mass, like the large clouds in the sky. They have no form to them; they are just floating along. The second word for cloud in the Greek is *nethalie,* which is found in 1 Thessalonians 4 and this word means a definitely shaped cloud, or a mass of clouds that possess a definite form. These are the clouds that we see that are with Christ, and we will be caught up in these clouds. So the word "cloud" in this passage is totally different from the one in Hebrews 12:1. They are not even the same word in the Greek text. They mean something completely different.

The other phrase in question in verse 17 is "caught up," and though the word "rapture" doesn't occur in the King James—or any Bible for that matter—the phrase "caught up" means "rapture." The word in the Greek is *harpadzo,* which is transliterated into Latin to the word *rapturo* from which we get our word "rapture." It simply means to be caught up suddenly, snatched away by force, or snatched away from danger, and the Lord is very explicit here in reference to the chronological order of events. It all takes place exactly as 1 Thessalonians 4 says. The Lord is going to come back, we are going to be changed in a moment, in the twinkling of an eye, and then we will be caught up together with the risen dead in the clouds to meet the Lord in the air, "and so shall we ever be with the Lord." This is the chronological order of events that takes place, it is *not* the same event as His Second Coming at the end of the Tribulation period. The Rapture takes place prior to the Tribulation.

Going back to the "clouds," we do not know exactly what these clouds are. We do know that the angelic communications, or angelic traffic, or traffic of God in the heavens, is referred to in many scriptures. In Psalm 68:17 we read: "The chariots of God are twenty thousand, even thousands of angels: the Lord is among them, as in Sinai, in the holy place." In this verse angels are associated with the chariots of God. The chariots of God are twenty thousand, or even thousands, meaning they are innumerable. We don't know what the chariots of God are.

In Isaiah 66:15 we read about the Lord's literal return at the end of the Tribulation:

> For, behold, the LORD will come with fire, and with his chariots like a whirlwind, to render his anger with fury, and his rebuke with flames of fire.

We remember that Elijah was caught up in a whirling, fiery chariot. We don't know what kind of celestial transportation apparatus, or vehicle, caught Elijah up. All we are told is that he was caught up in a fiery chariot. We read in Matthew 17 that on the Mount of Transfiguration when the Lord revealed to the apostles how He would look when He would come into His Kingdom at His Second Coming, that Elijah and Moses came out of a cloud on the Mount of Transfiguration, then they went back up into heaven in a cloud. On the Mount of Olives Jesus disappeared in a cloud. We are not trying to read something into this that isn't there, but only trying to shed as much light as possible on this particular meaning in 1 Thessalonians 4 about how we are going to be caught up, how we are going to be changed, how we are going to be raptured. It encompasses a translation, a change, a resurrection, then a transportation, or a catching away up into heavenly places, "and so shall we ever be with the Lord."

As we have noted, in the epistles to the churches there is not much said about angels. Take the Gospel of John, for example. The Gospel of John is the only one of the gospels that is silent on the ministry of angels. Angels are only mentioned four times in the Gospel of John, and these only in a peripheral meaning or sense. Why would John mention angels only four times with vague references in his gospel? Because his gospel was written in A.D. 90 when the Temple had already been destroyed, and the offer of the Kingdom had been completely withdrawn. There was no possible way then that Israel could repent at that time and call out to God. They had been scattered into the nations; probably two-thirds of Israel had been killed or sent into slavery. The Gospel of John was written mainly to the Church. If we didn't have the Gospel of John then we would really have some problems correlating the other three gospels with the epistles to the Church.

We again come to these questions: Why would Matthew, Mark, Luke, and John each write a gospel? Why would each one be different in some aspects, although they all correlate or reconcile in others? How would these men after thirty, forty, sixty years remember what Jesus said? Those are some of the criticisms that so-called biblical authorities present to cast doubt upon the Scriptures. We know that Jesus told them in John 16:13 the Holy Spirit would guide them. So, the writers of the gospels were under direct control of the Holy Spirit.

John does not mention angels at all in his epistles. His epistles were also written in about A.D. 90. But when we come to the Book of Revelation, what do we find? Why would John suddenly start mentioning angels in almost every verse? In the Book of Revelation, which he wrote in A.D. 96, there are sixty-eight references to angels. Why, when John had ignored the ministry of angels in his gospels and his epistles, would he suddenly in the Book of Revelation start mentioning angels over and over and over again in almost every chapter? Because, again, the Kingdom is in view here. The Church is gone. During this age we are depending upon the Holy Spirit. Our bodies are the temple of the Holy Spirit. The Holy Spirit leads us in what God wants us to do as long as we are obedient to His will. But, during the Tribulation, the Holy Spirit is taken out of the world. Here we see again the abundant and immense increase in the ministry of angels during the Tribulation period. This is just another reason why we do not see the Church at all in the Tribulation period.

The first time that angels are seen in the Book of Revelation is in the first verse of chapter one:

> The Revelation of Jesus Christ, which God gave unto him, to shew unto his servants things which must shortly come to pass; and he sent and signified it by his angel unto his servant John.

Again, God begins to work through angels. We, as Christians, are instructed by the Holy Spirit. God does not deal with Israel or the unsaved directly. He works through His angels.

In chapters two and three we find the angels to the seven churches in Asia. The messages to the churches are one of the most difficult sections in the Bible to place dispensationally. There were doubtless those congregations in A.D. 96 in Turkey. We have been to all of the sites of these churches. There aren't any churches there now. Turkey is a very strict Moslem country, one of the strictest and most oppressive—other faiths and religions simply are not tolerated.

As we look at the messages to the churches and the angels being over them, whether they be literally angels of God or messengers of the Church, we see here types of churches. Some place these churches as representative of different Church ages. For example, the church at Smyrna, from A.D. 100 to 300, a period of great persecution; the message to Pergamos, a period when the Church joined the world about 300 to 500. We could go on and on down to the end-time of the rich church. But as we look at these seven different churches, we can see the same churches today, the same types of churches. Repeatedly in these messages to the churches we find the words, "I will come upon you"; "I will not cast you into tribulation or let you endure the time of great temptation"; "I will come upon you in my wrath." So, there may have been churches, and probably were, in all of these seven cities. They may represent the different Church ages (although we may have a problem with this explanation), but we know that there are all types of these seven churches in the world today: the rich church, the overabundant church, the apostate church, the great whore church, the Jezebel church, etc.

The next time that angels are mentioned is in chapter four, verses 6 through 8:

> And before the throne there was a sea of glass like unto crystal: and in the midst of the throne, and round about the throne, were four beasts full of eyes before and behind. And the first beast was like a lion, and the second beast like a calf, and the third beast had a face as a man, and the fourth beast was like a flying eagle. And the four beasts had each of them six wings about him; and they were full of eyes within: and they rest not day and night, saying, Holy, holy, holy, Lord God Almighty, which was, and is, and is to come.

The veil in the Temple of God in heaven is lifted so that

the Apostle John receives a glimpse of the order of government in the Kingdom of God. In our next chapter we will consider more closely the delegated authority of the angelic cherubim who guard the various orders of God's creation.

X.

War of the Angels

We have now advanced in our study up to the Tribulation period. From Genesis all the way through the books of the Old Testament, through the dispensation of innocence, the dispensation of conscience, the dispensation of human government, of law, of grace, we now come to the time when the Church is raptured, taken out of the world, and the ministry of angels once more becomes prominent.

We read much in the four gospels about the ministry of angels, because Jesus was offering the Kingdom of Heaven. He came preaching, "Repent, for the kingdom of heaven is at hand." So did John the Baptist. The ministry of angels is also prevalent in the Book of Acts up to about the thirteenth chapter because the Kingdom was still being offered. But then we get to the Church Age, when the Church came into its fullness with the conversion of Paul—Paul was sent to be an apostle to the Gentiles—we see the ministry of angels becoming less in evidence.

John wrote his gospel in A.D. 90 and was not too concerned in his gospel about the ministry of angels. In fact, he only mentioned angels four times on a peripheral basis in his entire gospel. John did not mention angels at all in his epistles, but now we come to the Book of Revelation. John wrote the Book of Revelation in A.D. 96, and in his vision, he was transported in the Spirit into the time of the Great Tribulation. The Church Age is over;

the Church is gone; the ministry of the Holy Spirit in the world in the lives of individual Christians has ceased. Sixty-eight times John mentions angels in the Book of Revelation.

In Revelation 4:6, the four living creatures are presented as cherubim. They have been mentioned previously as the angels, or watchers, who watch over the whole creation of living things, including men, birds, domestic animals, and wild animals. There is no mention of an angel watching over the reptiles, but in Habakkuk we read that these creatures have no angel over them. Some believe that Satan, as Lucifer, may have been a watcher over the creeping things and reptiles, but he fell.

The next time that angels are mentioned is in Revelation 5:2, and we read:

> And I saw a strong angel proclaiming with a loud voice, Who is worthy to open the book, and to loose the seals thereof?

Here we see Jesus Christ as the only One Who is capable of, or strong enough, or has the ability to open this seven-sealed book to begin this Tribulation period. It can be seen in verses 5 and 6 that the Father Himself is holding this seal, and this angel is a strong angel. This word "strong" here has the connotation that he is powerful; he has a specific task to do. Who he is, is not known. He is just an angel that has been assigned this particular task to do. The angels of God are not working independently of Him, and that can be seen throughout this study. The angels of God work at *His* command. Satan's angels also have a particular task to do, which is to thwart the work of God. But here we see the strong angel proclaiming, "Who is able to open this seven-sealed book?" As we read in the text, it is Christ Himself. There is none other that is powerful enough to do it.

The next time that angels appear is in Revelation 8:2. In Revelation 8:2 we see seven angels of judgment.

> And when he had opened the seventh seal, there was silence in heaven about the space of half an hour. And I saw the seven angels which stood before God; and to them were given seven trumpets (vss. 1–2).

As the angels blow the trumpets, judgments come upon the world. During the ministry of Christ it is indicated that if He had wanted to, He could have called angels down at the cross, or when He was insulted, or spit upon, or when He was arrested in the garden of Gethsemane. At any time He could have called avenging angels, but the angels were restrained at that time. They have also been restrained during the dispensation of grace. But here in Revelation, finally, the angels are restrained no longer. We see seven angels come forth to bring seven trumpets, and as each angel blows a trumpet it starts a series of judgments upon the earth to redeem earth from the control and authority of Satan and unregenerate men.

We can certainly praise God that we who are Christians will not be on earth during this time of Great Tribulation, a time that Jesus said would be so terrible that there had never been a time like it before, and there would never be a time like it again.

In Revelation 10:1 we read:

> And I saw another mighty angel come down from heaven, clothed with a cloud: and a rainbow was upon his head, and his face was as it were the sun, and his feet as pillars of fire.

The word "mighty" is the same word in the Greek that we see in Revelation 5:2 where it is rendered "strong." Is it possible that these two angels are the same? We don't know if these two angels are the same or not, but each has a particular task to do. Here he is introducing to John the little book and asks him to eat it. We see the connotation there that he took the book and ate it, and it made his "belly bitter" but in his "mouth sweet as honey."

In Revelation 11:1–2 we read:

> And there was given me a reed like unto a rod: and the angel stood, saying, Rise, and measure the temple of God, and the altar, and them that worship therein. But the court which is without the temple leave out, and measure it not; for it is given unto the Gentiles: and the holy city shall they tread under foot forty and two months [three and one-half years].

This may be something that is going to happen at the middle of the Tribulation period. This concerns the Temple the Antichrist will defile. The religious Jews in Israel today are zealous about rebuilding the Temple. Even nominal religious Jews are interested in building the Temple. During a recent trip to Israel we saw thousands of Jews before the Western Wall praying and lighting candles during Hanukkah, praying for God to make it possible to rebuild the Temple. Nearby yeshivas are training priests to resume Temple worship, and weaving priests clothing, and making articles of furnishings for the Temple. Many Israelis are putting forth great efforts to restore Temple worship.

Through some kind of peace arrangement Israel will be permitted to build a Temple again, but it will not be a house of God according to biblical or spiritual specifications. So, an angel will come down to measure the Temple, and to see if it fits the requirements for the house of God. We know that there is only one house of God, the Lord's house, as far as a physical structure, and that was the Temple in Jerusalem. During this dispensation Christians are the temple of the Holy Spirit, but when this temple is removed (the Church), we see another temple—a physical temple—again coming into view even as it was when Jesus was here on earth. So this angel comes down to measure the temple, and the angel finds that this temple does not meet the requirements. We read on that the Beast, the Antichrist, will stand in this temple showing himself to the whole world that he is God. This act will start the Abomination of Desolation and the last half of the Tribulation.

Revelation 12 is one of the most interesting chapters in the Book of Revelation, and we see here a scene halfway through the Tribulation period (three and one-half years into the Tribulation period) where Satan is being cast out of heaven. No longer will he have access to the throne of God as he has had in the past. He and his host (those angels who follow him) are being literally, and physically perhaps, cast out of heaven. In verse 7 we read of the one who leads the charge against Satan and his angels:

> And there was war in heaven: Michael and his angels fought against the dragon; and the dragon fought and his angels.

Michael is in charge of a particular number of angels, perhaps one-third, or the same number that Lucifer is in charge of. But we see something unusual here, in that Michael takes on a different disposition than he had in Jude, where we read:

Yet Michael the archangel, when contending with the
devil he disputed about the body of Moses, durst not
bring against him a railing accusation, but said, The
Lord rebuke thee (vs. 9).

This proves that Michael is *not* a loose cannon, per se, but
that he takes his orders from God and does God's bidding.
Here he is fighting against Satan by the authority given to
him by God Himself. Michael prevails, Satan and his angels
are cast down to the earth, and now Satan knows his time
is short and he sets about in desperation to do his work.
He possesses the Antichrist. The Antichrist goes into the
temple and proclaims himself to be God. The scenario
here is that angels are fighting. Angels of God with Michael
fighting against the angels of Satan in a cosmic war.
    The next place that angels are mentioned is in
Revelation 14:6–7:

And I saw another angel fly in the midst of heaven,
having the everlasting gospel to preach unto them that
dwell on the earth, and to every nation, and kindred,
and tongue, and people, Saying with a loud voice, Fear
God, and give glory to him; for the hour of his judgment
is come: and worship him that made heaven, and earth,
and the sea, and the fountains of waters.

We see here the seventh angel again, and he is proclaiming
the "everlasting gospel." This is the gospel that God gave
Adam and Eve: to fear God and to keep His
commandments, and to give Him honor as Creator. The
thing that humanity is rejecting today—the kings, the
nations, the scientists, the humanists, the agnostics—is
that God is Creator, who created all things in heaven and
earth. That is what mankind is rebelling against today.

This is the truth that the nations (humanity) are rejecting, but God never leaves the unsaved without a witness before judgment comes. Even though there is no witness left in the world, another angel flies "in the midst of heaven" with the everlasting gospel, warning those left alive to give God the glory and worship Him as Creator before judgment falls. We believe this is the final warning given to the world during the Tribulation period before the great and last judgment comes, and there is no hope left for those who reject God and worship Satan and his christ. Angels can preach the gospel because Paul said that if an angel from heaven preach another gospel, "let him be accursed." But here an angel comes with the everlasting gospel giving mankind the last invitation to repent and be saved before the day of God's wrath comes.

The next angel is found in Revelation 14:14. We have here a picture of the battle of Armageddon. Verse 15:

> And another angel came out of the temple, crying with a loud voice to him that sat on the cloud, Thrust in thy sickle, and reap: for the time is come for thee to reap; for the harvest of the earth is ripe.

The angel is proclaiming to the person sitting on the cloud, which we see in verse 14 to be Christ Himself, that it is time for Him to thrust in the sickle to begin the battle of Armageddon, which He does. He does thrust in the sickle, and in verse 20 we read:

> And the winepress was trodden without the city, and blood came out of the winepress, even unto the horse bridles, by the space of a thousand and six hundred furlongs."

We were recently in Israel at Megiddo, and viewed the valley, and what a vast plain it is. Napoleon said, as he stood and overlooked this valley from Megiddo, that all the armies of the world could marshal here for a battle. This battle is going to happen. This battle will occur at the end of the Tribulation period.

The next place we see angels mentioned is in Revelation 14:9–10:

> And the third angel followed them, saying with a loud voice, If any man worship the beast and his image, and receive his mark in his forehead, or in his hand, The same shall drink of the wine of the wrath of God, which is poured out without mixture into the cup of his indignation; and he shall be tormented with fire and brimstone in the presence of the holy angels, and in the presence of the Lamb.

Those who take the mark of the Beast, whether in the hand or the forehead, will suffer hell; the torment of fire and brimstone. They will not only suffer "in the presence of the Lamb," Jesus Christ, but also "in the presence of the holy angels." At the close of Revelation 13 we are told that the Antichrist will *demand* that everyone in the world take his mark and his number in their hand or in their forehead. This is a sign that they have accepted *him* as their christ, though he is the Antichrist; he is Satan's christ. Anyone who takes this mark wears a sign that they have utterly rejected Jesus Christ. It is not just the mark that is going to send them to hell, it is the fact that they have accepted this man as their christ and rejected Jesus Christ. All those who take the mark during the Tribulation period will be cast into the lake of fire, an eternal hell. The third angel then comes and warns those who are on the earth. First, an angel comes and tells them how to be saved, then this angel follows that angel and warns the world that if they take the mark of the Beast—the mark of Antichrist—they will endure eternal judgment.

Angels during the Tribulation not only have a ministry of judgment; they have a ministry of salvation, to warn the world against the Antichrist and the fate of those who accept the Antichrist as their god.

XI.

Avenging Angels

The ministry of angels becomes prevalent again in the Book of Revelation, because the Book of Revelation deals with a change in dispensation. The gospel of grace is over, and Jesus directly intervenes to bring all nations and all things under His power and authority. The age of God's grace is over. Now comes the age of judgment, the time of judgment which is the great and terrible day of God's wrath. As brought out before, God never leaves mankind without a hope, without an invitation, without a message of salvation, without a way of escape. He provided a way of escape before the flood; He had a way of escape at Sodom and Gomorrah; He always has a way of escape for those who will receive His message of salvation, just as He does today. There is a way for anyone to escape the judgment of an eternal hell, and that is to receive Jesus Christ as Lord and Savior.

As we look at the ministry of angels during the Tribulation as set forth in the Book of Revelation, we have now advanced to seven additional angels of judgment, the angels with the seven vials. In Revelation 15:1 we read:

> And I saw another sign in heaven, great and marvellous, seven angels having the seven last plagues; for in them is filled up the wrath of God.

God is about to unleash His wrath, His plagues upon the

earth, and nothing will be spared. Each one of these seven angels has a different vial. In chapter sixteen, verse 1, we read about the "wrath of God." The wrath of God is about to be poured out upon earth. We see in the following verses in chapter sixteen that the first vial was poured out upon the earth (vs. 2), then in verse 4 "the third angel poured out his vial upon the rivers and fountains of waters." Then in verse 8 God's wrath is poured out upon the sun, and in verse 10 "the fifth angel poured out his vial upon the seat of the beast; and his kingdom was full of darkness." Then in verse 12 the plague was poured out on the river Euphrates. Nothing is spared; there is no place to hide; no place to go. The last vial is poured out into the air (vs. 17). So, there is nothing that escapes the wrath of God. The next place that angels are mentioned is in Revelation 17—the angels with the seven dooms.

Revelation 17 introduces the angels with the seven dooms. In the Pilgrim Bible it says "the seven dooms," although these seven dooms are not enumerated here, they are contained within the context of this particular judgment. In Revelation 17:1 we read this:

> And there came one of the seven angels which had the seven vials, and talked with me, saying unto me, Come hither; I will shew unto thee the judgment of the great whore that sitteth upon many waters.

The angels with the seven dooms refer primarily to the judgment of the false religious system of the Tribulation. Here we see a woman coming forth on a beast, a political beast. The religious system comes riding in on a political beast. In all theocratic systems of religion the political system upholds the religious system, and the religious system upholds the political system. That was the arrangement in the Holy Roman Empire when the pope gave ecclesiastic authority to the kings to rule over the nations. That will be the kind of arrangement that is going to be in effect during the Tribulation period. This false religious system is going to be judged by the angels, and then destroyed by the angels. The angels are certainly going to have an important part in destroying the false religious system of the Tribulation period. This is the Antichrist's church; this is the religion of Satan in which he deceives the whole world. All of those whose names are not written in the Lamb's Book of Life during the Tribulation period will belong to this church. Of course, we know that some will escape because Jesus said unless those days should be shortened, there would no flesh be saved. But it is going to be a terrible time here on earth when the angels come to judge the false religious system of the Tribulation period

In chapter eighteen we see the economic fall of Babylon. Revelation 18:1–2 reads:

> And after these things I saw another angel come down from heaven, having great power; and the earth was lightened with his glory. And he cried mightily with a strong voice, saying, Babylon the great is fallen, is fallen, and is become the habitation of devils, and the hold of every foul spirit, and a cage of every unclean and hateful bird.

John explained that this system is against God. God warns His people to come out of it and stay out of it because He is going to destroy it.

We have been to Babylon. Saddam Hussein has restored the old Babylon of Nebuchadnezzar. In fact, the bricks that he used in some of the reconstruction had his name on one end, and Nebuchadnezzar's name on the other end. Although mainly rebuilt for a tourist site, Babylon has pretty much been restored. We read in Jeremiah 50–52, that God has reserved total judgment for two entities, or two nations. These are the nations that destroyed the Temple: Babylon and the Revived Roman Empire. Neither of these national entities were destroyed like Sodom and Gomorrah previously. Babylon was simply vacated and buried under sand; it was never destroyed like Sodom and Gomorrah. Neither was the Roman Empire destroyed like Sodom and Gomorrah. We read that the seat of the Beast, or the capitol of the Roman Empire, will be destroyed also like Sodom and Gomorrah. So, God has reserved judgment for two national entities: Babylon and the Roman Empire (or the Revived Roman Empire) that will be destroyed ultimately like Sodom and Gomorrah. We read here that angels will have an important part in the destruction of both of these national entities. We read in Revelation 19:17–18 of an appeal:

> And I saw an angel standing in the sun; and he cried with a loud voice, saying to all the fowls that fly in the midst of heaven, Come and gather yourselves together unto the supper of the great God; That ye may eat the flesh of kings, and the flesh of captains. . . .

According to the description of the battle of Armageddon it will rage from Megiddo all the way down to Basra in Jordan, which is the gateway to Petra; 1,600 furlongs. That's 176 miles. The angel comes to announce that the battle of Armageddon has occurred. There are hundreds of thousands of men now dead on the plains all over Israel from Megiddo, probably all the way down to the Dead Sea, and then on in to Jordan. So, the angel calls the fowls of heaven.

When Israel was out of her land, it was barren. All the trees, and even the grass was gone. All the animals left, and because there were no animals there for the buzzards or birds of prey to eat, they left also. Now, however, all the animals mentioned in the Bible are again in Israel. We were in Gamla and there was an ibex that some animal had killed; a wolf or perhaps a leopard. The vultures had picked the bones of this ibex clean, and there was not a bit of meat left on it. Now when you go to Gamla you see the buzzards flying up and down the ravine. The birds of prey are back. The stage is set for this scene here in Revelation.

We know that when Jesus comes back, as we read in Isaiah 66, that God is going to send His chariots whirling like chariots of fire, and the angels will come with Him. They will overthrow the armies of Antichrist in the Middle East, and this will do away with the authority of Gentile power over the world. Then the stage is set for Jesus Christ to set up His own Kingdom here on earth, His Kingdom of Heaven, and reign upon the throne of David.

The angel announces the battle of Armageddon and calls the birds of prey, the vultures, the eagles, to gather on the plains of Megiddo all the way down past Jerusalem, the Kidron Valley, and all the way down into Jordan. It is now time for God to fulfill His covenant to Abraham that the land that Abraham's feet passed over would finally be claimed by his seed, the nation of Israel, the descendants of Abraham through Isaac.

How are the Jews left alive in the world going to be regathered back into Israel? Matthew 24:31 speaks of the end of the Tribulation period:

And he shall send his angels with a great sound of a trumpet, and they shall gather together his elect from the four winds, from one end of heaven to the other.

This is a period of time immediately after the Tribulation period. The entire Tribulation period will last seven years, but there will be a transitional period, evidently at the beginning of the Millennium. We read in Daniel 12:11:

> And from the time that the daily sacrifice shall be taken away, and the abomination that maketh desolate set up, there shall be a thousand two hundred and ninety days.

We know that the second half of the Tribulation period is going to be 1,260, so thirty days are added to the end of the Tribulation period. Then in verse 12 we read:

> Blessed is he that waiteth, and cometh to the thousand three hundred and five and thirty days.

An extra forty-five days is added to the thirty days. That is an additional seventy-five days between the Tribulation period and the Millennium. Then Daniel is told in verse 13:

> But go thou thy way till the end be: for thou shalt rest, and stand in thy lot at the end of the days.

We read in Matthew 25:31–32:

> When the Son of man shall come in his glory, and all the holy angels with him, then shall he sit upon the throne of his glory: And before him shall be gathered all nations: and he shall separate them one from another, as a shepherd divideth his sheep from the goats.

What do we really see here in this time period? (We are

looking here at the end of the Tribulation period after the battle of Armageddon when the armies of the Antichrist have been defeated; the armies of the Beast have been slain; the Antichrist and the false prophet cast into the lake of fire.) We know that from the start of the Tribulation period to the end of the Tribulation period is going to be seven years, or two periods of three and one-half years. The last half, we're told, is going to be 1,260 days. Then we have a period of thirty days, which brings us to thirty days beyond the battle of Armageddon. What we have here during this time is the regathering of Israel. We're told in Matthew 24:31 that Jesus is going to send the angels to gather the children of Israel; the elect. The elect here are the Israelites who are left alive at the end of the Tribulation period. We know that during the Tribulation period that two-thirds in the land will be killed, and one-third will be brought through the fire. But in Matthew 24:31 we read:

> And he shall send his angels with a great sound of a trumpet, and they shall gather together his elect from the four winds, from one end of heaven to the other.

This refers to any Jew, or Israelite, who is left alive at the end of the Tribulation period. In Amos 9:2–3 we have some further insight into this particular time:

> Though they dig into hell, thence shall mine hand take them; though they climb up to heaven, thence will I bring them down: And though they hide themselves in the top of Carmel, I will search and take them out thence; and though they be hid from my sight in the bottom of the sea, thence will I command the serpent, and he shall bite them.

So, even if there are any Jews in submarines at that time, though there be any Jews in mines, though there be any Jews in any space vehicle on their way to Mars, the Word here states that God will bring every one of them back into the land, and there He will judge them. Those that receive Him and believe on Him will be saved. We read in the Book of Romans that they will look upon Him Whom they have pierced. The Deliverer shall roar out of Zion, and all in Israel who look upon Him, and receive Him as not only the Messiah, but the One Who died for their sins, those will be saved.

During this period of thirty days it is apparent that the Jews will be regathered back into the land. We read here that this will be done by the angels. The angels will gather them back. Now we come to an extra period of forty-five days, or 1,335 days. The last half of the Tribulation is extended another forty-five days. What are the forty-five days for? We don't know exactly the reason for the extra forty-five days, except perhaps that this is the time that Jesus will set up His Kingdom here on earth.

In Revelation 20:1, we read:

> And I saw an angel come down from heaven, having the key of the bottomless pit and a great chain in his hand.

Then on down in verse 4 we read:

> And I saw thrones, and they sat upon them, and judgment [or authority] was given unto them. . . .

A government is going to be set up and there will be thrones. Jesus promised the twelve apostles that they would sit upon twelve thrones judging the twelve tribes of Israel. Jesus is going to set up His Kingdom. Then we have His government ruling the nations. In Matthew 25:31–32 we read:

> When the Son of man shall come in his glory, and all the holy angels with him, then shall he sit upon the throne of his glory [this is the throne of David]: And before him shall be gathered all nations: and he shall separate them one from another, as a shepherd divideth his sheep from the goats.

This scripture refers to the government of Jesus Christ being set up to rule over all the nations during the Millennium. The scenario is as follows: Jesus comes back at the battle of Armageddon with all His angels; the armies of Antichrist and the false prophet will be destroyed; the Antichrist and the false prophet are cast into the lake of fire; and the angels go throughout all the world gathering the seed of Abraham (the seed of Israel through Isaac) who are left alive. Of course, Jesus also warned that some would be thrown into outer darkness, and that there would be wailing and gnashing of teeth. But every Jew, every Israelite, will be given an opportunity to look upon Him Whom they, meaning Israel, have pierced. In that day they will all be given an opportunity to be saved at the end of the Tribulation period. This is not a second chance after death. This involves a commitment that God has made to them. God has a covenant with Israel that He will take away their sins. Those who look upon Him Whom they have pierced, receive Him as their Messiah, the One Who died for their sins, will be saved.

After this comes the judgment of the nations; the ruling of the nations during the Millennium in which Jesus will sit upon the throne of His glory and He will rule the nations with a rod of iron. This refers to His millennial reign after the Tribulation period.

XII.

Angels in the Millennium

In this chapter we will study the ministry of angels during the Millennium, the thousand-year reign of Christ. What are the angels going to be doing during the Millennium? What is going to happen immediately after the battle of Armageddon when Jesus Christ establishes His Kingdom from heaven on this earth?

We've considered in our study up to this point angelic activity under the law of the Old Testatment, through the gospels of the New Testament, and the formation of the Church in the first century. Then we see a lull in the activity of angels during the Church Age. This may be because of the witness of the Holy Spirit, or the indwelling ministry of the Holy Spirit. It seems like they have been—more or less—relegated to be witnesses, or in a state of observation. We've gone all the way through the Tribulation period where they are once again very, very active, and now we go into the Millennium, the thousand-year reign of Christ. Immediately we see that there is a big change. In Revelation 20:2–3 John says:

> And he [an angel] laid hold on the dragon, that old serpent, which is the Devil, and Satan, and bound him a thousand years, And cast him into the bottomless pit, and shut him up, and set a seal upon him, that he should deceive the nations no more, till the thousand years

should be fulfilled: and after that he must be loosed a little season.

For the first time since the Garden of Eden, we see that Satan is not going to be on earth to deceive, either on an individual basis, or national basis, nor will he be here to lead the fallen angels which followed him. We see something very, very different.

In the Book of Revelation, especially in chapter 20, we do not receive much insight into what is going to happen to Satan's angels. We know from Revelation 12 that Satan and his angels will be cast down to the earth; cast out of the heavenlies onto the earth. When Satan and the false prophet are cast into the lake of fire, where are his angels? How is God going to deal with his angels? We have some insight into the state of fallen angels during the Millennium from Isaiah 24. If we want to know more about the Millennium we go to the Old Testament, because many of the promises to Israel in the Old Testament look forward to the Millennium. As far as Satan's angels, we read in Isaiah 24:21–23:

> And it shall come to pass in that day [the Millennium],
> that the LORD shall punish the host of the high ones
> that are on high [Satan and his angels will be cast down],
> and the kings of the earth upon the earth [this is the
> Tribulation, and these are days following the
> Tribulation]. And they shall be gathered together, as
> prisoners are gathered in the pit, and shall be shut up
> in the prison, and after many days shall they be visited.

Satan's angels are going to be shut up in the bottomless pit for a thousand years along with Satan. So, Satan and his angels are going to be cast into the bottomless pit.

But, it also says here that "after many days shall they be visited." What does this relate to? It relates to "a little season" found in Revelation 20:3. This is the same time period. According to Scripture they will be imprisoned for one thousand years, the exact length of time that Satan, their leader, is bound. Then they will be released at the same time as Satan at the end of the Millennium to regather his forces for the battle of Gog and Magog. In Revelation 20:7–8 we read:

> And when the thousand years are expired [this is during the Millennium], Satan shall be loosed out of his prison, And shall go out to deceive the nations. . . .

According to Isaiah, Satan is going to be loosed, and his angels are going to be loosed with him. So, Satan and his angels are bound for a thousand years during the Millennium, but at the end of the Millennium they will be loosed and, according to the scripture, they will go forth to deceive the nations, and lead the nations of the world once again against the Lord Jesus Christ and His government in Jerusalem. Then in Revelation 20:10 we read:

> And the devil that deceived them was cast into the lake of fire and brimstone, where the beast and the false prophet are, and shall be tormented day and night for ever and ever.

According to Isaiah, and other scriptures that we could refer to, it appears that when Satan is finally cast into the lake of fire, his angels will also be cast into the lake of fire with him. Neither will the Devil or his angels be able to torment or deceive the world any more. Now, what about the angels of God during the Millennium?

The angels of God are evidently going to be very active. We read in Matthew 25:31–34:

> When the Son of man shall come in his glory, and all the holy angels with him [they are all going to come and attend the Lord as He comes to sit on His throne], then shall he sit upon the throne of his glory: And before him shall be gathered all nations: and he shall separate them one from another, as a shepherd divideth his sheep from the goats: And he shall set the sheep on his right hand, but the goats on the left. Then shall the King say unto them on his right hand, Come, ye blessed of my Father, inherit the kingdom prepared for you from the foundation of the world.

We see here, as always, Christ is going to use His angels to accompany Him and to be messengers for Him as He judges and rules the nations. When does this judgment take place?

The Scofield and Pilgrim Bibles refer national judgment to the conclusion of the Tribulation period, or after the battle of Armageddon Jesus gathers all nations and judges them at that time. But we read that He sits "upon the throne of his glory, And before him shall be gathered all nations." In other scriptures we know that He will rule the nations with a rod of iron. It will be His government, and He will rule the nations during the thousand years, and it would appear that this judgment of the nations is a continuing process over the thousand-year reign of Christ, and the final judgment of the nations is included in the Great White Throne Judgment.

If we look at Matthew 25, the concluding verses:

> Then shall he answer them, saying, Verily I say unto

you, Inasmuch as ye did it not to one of the least of these [meaning His brethren], ye did it not to me. And these shall go away into everlasting punishment: but the righteous into life eternal.

This is not a Millennial judgment, but a Great White Throne judgment. The judgment mentioned here in Matthew 25 of the nations, is a continuing process that concludes at the Great White Throne Judgment. Some may disagree, but this is our understanding.

In any event, we know that the angels are going to be very active in the administration of Jesus Christ, the great King, during the Millennium. We read that if Egypt doesn't come up to the Feast of Tabernacles that no rain will come upon Egypt. We read that a sinner being one hundred years old, if he doesn't repent, he'll be cut off; that means he'll be killed; executed. So, the angels will have an important part in the administration of Jesus Christ here on earth during the Millennium.

That brings up a very interesting point. Many people believe that if it were not for Satan and his angels there would be no sin committed, because no one would be enticed to sin. In the Millennium we see that Christ is going to rule with a rod of iron, which means that there is going to be sin. Now, since Satan and his angels are bound at this particular time, why will people continue to sin? It is because of the sin nature of man. What Satan does or does not do, does not affect the sin nature. Even if there were no Devil, because of our sin nature, we would still sin. Some people would ask: "Well, why a Millennium anyway?" During the Millennium Satan will be bound; his angels will be bound; there will be a perfect King; there will be a perfect government; there will be plenty. People can't say, "I didn't have food. That's why I went out and killed"; or, "We had a corrupt government, therefore this is why we have so much trouble and sin in the world. If we just had a good government there wouldn't be so much crime. If we just had food there wouldn't be so much crime." All this is going to be proven an error in the Millennium; that it is the sin nature within us, and whatever God does at the Great White Throne Judgment, He will be justified in doing it. Man will be accountable for his own sins. He can't blame anybody else or any other thing but himself. God must be justified. Why must God be justified? Because of Who He is, and what He is.

People will have no excuse at the conclusion of the Millennium. God will have proven His love and His justice and His omnipotent authority for ever and ever. No one in all eternity can blame God for anything, because God will have gone the very last mile, the very last year, the very last minute, the very last second, to redeem man from his sin, and in eternity He will have His people and His angels, those who have loved Him and served Him, not because they had to, but because they chose to.

Let us next consider the ministry of angels in the New Heaven and the New Earth. What will the ministry of angels be in the New Heaven and the New Earth? In Revelation 21:9–10 we read:

> And there came unto me one of the seven angels which had the seven vials full of the seven last plagues, and talked with me, saying, Come hither, I will shew thee the bride, the Lamb's wife. And he carried me away in the spirit to a great and high mountain, and shewed me that great city, the holy Jerusalem, descending out of heaven from God.

We see here in the new Jerusalem that the angels will be

present. The writer of Hebrews 12:22 says that in "the heavenly Jerusalem . . . an innumerable company of angels" will inherit it. Evidently, this means that angels will be living in new Jerusalem along with others who are the inhabitants thereof.

Angels are also mentioned in Revelation 21:12 where we read about the new Jerusalem, that it will have "a wall great and high," and "twelve gates, and at the gates twelve angels, and names written thereon, which are the names of the twelve tribes of the children of Israel." So, the new Jerusalem will have a great high wall with twelve gates, and on the gates there will be the names of the twelve tribes of Israel, and angels will be at the gates. Evidently, angels are going to have a very important ministry in the New Heaven and the New Earth. They will be part of God's heavenly government, and they will be guardians over the gates of the new Jerusalem.

There is one more reference to angels in Revelation 22. In chapter twenty-two we see the last message that John has for us, and the last angel mentioned in the Book of Revelation, and the Bible. In Revelation 22:8–9 we read:

> And I John saw these things, and heard them. And when I had heard and seen, I fell down to worship before the feet of the angel which shewed me these things. Then saith he unto me, See thou do it not: for I am thy fellowservant, and of thy brethren the prophets, and of them which keep the sayings of this book: worship God.

The angel gives John instructions about not sealing up the book, what is to take place prior to eternity, and the things involved in eternity, and who's not going to serve God in eternity. Jesus Christ concludes the Revelation:

And if any man shall take away from the words of the book of this prophecy, God shall take away his part out of the book of life, and out of the holy city, and from the things which are written in this book (Rev. 22:19).

The end result of Satan and his angels is described in Matthew 25:41, where we read:

Then shall he say also unto them on the left hand, Depart from me, ye cursed, into everlasting fire, prepared for the devil and his angels.

The lake of fire was made for the Devil and his angels, but because of sin and disobedience man will end up there also. When we sin and rebel against God, then we become part of Satan's kingdom. There are only two kingdoms in the world: the kingdom of the Devil, and the Kingdom of God. If you are born again, then you become children of God and members of His Kingdom. People will go to hell along with the Devil and his angels because they choose to, ignoring that God has made a way of escape.

In reference to the angel that John fell down to worship, the angel admonished him not to worship him. Why? Because "I am thy fellowservant." In 1 Corinthians 6:3 we read that Christians are going to judge angels. When will we judge angels? We believe that it is in the New Heaven and the New Earth. In the eternal Kingdom our place will be higher than that of the angels, and what a glorious heritage that is going to be, to know that God has elected and appointed us, and that in eternity we are going to be greater than the angels. We read in Ephesians that we are going to inherit heavenly places. Some people ask: "What about Israel?" I don't want any of Israel. I think there is a planet or a solar system or a galaxy out reserved for me. That's what I want. In eternity, when we inherit heavenly places, we're told that we are going to rule over the angels. With the angels, we will boldly go where no man has gone before.